Ungrading
The
Elementary
School

UNGRADING
THE
ELEMENTARY
SCHOOL

FRANK R. DUFAY

PARKER PUBLISHING COMPANY, Inc.
WEST NYACK, N. Y.

174492

372. 12
D 854

© 1966 BY

PARKER PUBLISHING COMPANY, INC.

WEST NYACK, N.Y.

ALL RIGHTS RESERVED. NO PART OF THIS BOOK
MAY BE REPRODUCED IN ANY FORM, BY
MIMEOGRAPH OR ANY OTHER MEANS, WITHOUT
PERMISSION IN WRITING FROM THE PUBLISHER

LIBRARY OF CONGRESS
CATALOG CARD NUMBER: 65-25232

PRINTED IN THE UNITED STATES OF AMERICA
93740—B&P

Dedication

To my wife Ann

and

my sons Frank Jr. and Paul

Acknowledgments

There can be no significant sequence in crediting the many people who have contributed in a variety of ways in the development of this book. Let me gratefully list them:

THE PARKWAY SCHOOL STAFF, whose efforts on behalf of children have brought credit to themselves and the district they serve . . .

THE PARKWAY COMMUNITY, for expressed confidence and support . . .

ROBERT F. SAVITT, a dynamic, inspiring superintendent of schools, a first-rate leader in the quest for quality education . . .

EDWARD J. DEJNOZKA, New York University's Director of the Virgin Islands Project, who, while chairman of my doctoral committee, devoted long hours in guiding the pursuit of more and better information . . .

WALTER CREWSON, Associate Commissioner of Education for New York State, who took time from a busy schedule to read through the manuscript in its early stages, making suggestions, and giving encouragement . . .

THE PERSONAL FRIENDS who kindly listened and reacted as I expressed the points of view to be found in this work . . .

THE FAMILY who endured the untidy clutter on the dining room table and who permitted Dad the nights of isolation.

Foreword

Stuart E. Dean

In 1959, when Goodlad and Anderson presented the first modern-day case for "The Nongraded School," another milestone in American education was reached. Since that day volumes and discussions have been abuilding on this captivating innovation in school organization. Understandably the focus of deliberations during the earlier years of the movement has been both on demonstrating the need for and on developing the underlying rationale of nongradedness. Primary emphasis has been properly placed upon interpreting a philosophic concept and on conveying a realization that only through programs of individualized, continuous pupil progress can our schools meet the challenges of the day.

Now we move on to another phase. In setting the stage for his report Dr. Dufay submits: "Thus, while many front-line educators are poised in readiness for the adventure that has been so extravagently and glowingly portrayed, they are restrained by a natural reluctance to move forward in relative darkness. They may know *why,* but they wish, also, to know *how.*" Therefore, it is logical and fitting that an evolutionary account of this nature now appears. For this book is intended to meet the needs of those who have been assimilating the message of nongradedness, of those who have been

13

involved in various stages of readiness and of preparation, and of those who are ready to move into action.

The author resists the temptation of intimating there are prescribed methods or procedures for all schools or that there is but one path to success in nongrading a school. In contrast, his is a modest, factual statement of how one school—Parkway, in Central School District #4, Plainview-old-Bethpage—of suburban Long Island, has gone about the task. Successes and failures, triumphs and defeats, progressions and regressions are recounted with candor and with frankness. The purpose of the book is, as the author puts it, "to share successful practices." It is a pragmatic recounting of a "working program."

To accomplish this purpose the book centers on the development of planning details and operational specifics. It deals with items which necessarily have been treated as generalities in prior discussions. For the past half dozen years writers and observers have been pointing out possible precautions, pitfalls, and hazards. For example, in undertaking nongradedness a school faces a number of important, early determinations, such as: basic grouping policy; methods of reporting pupil progress; securing community involvement and support; indoctrination and training of staff; and adjusting curriculum to continuous progress. Other common and knotty problems are discussed, such as: the inherent restrictions which stem from a subconscious commitment to "graded" thinking; the widespread practice of mere substitution of reading levels for grade levels in the naive assumption that this results in a nongraded school; and the changing role and responsibilities of the teacher in the nongraded school. Because of the opportunity this book provides to share in the experiences one school has had with some of the difficult and complex operational procedures it is to be hoped that others may be spared some of the more common abuses and misuses of the nongraded concept.

Of particular value are the writer's commentaries on "Action for Change." Within this context the urgency and need for a reclarification of elementary school goals and for the development of professional objectives are forcefully developed. Against a backdrop of analysis of the impact of change upon our schools the need for the nongraded school is forcibly demonstrated. From a discussion of the range and social significance of human variability the failures of the graded school are pointed out and the feasibility of individualized, continuous progress plans is developed. From examination of the need for flexibility of operation—people, space, and time— the parallel need for a "team" concept is drawn.

Thus, the spirit of the book is geared to practicality; how to operate a viable program. The actual steps, for example, of how the Parkway School set about solving the perplexing and perennial problems of grouping are first hand testimony of what a faculty is likely to go through. In similar manner, the use of subject specialists, ways of gaining community support, the role of the building principal are but a few of the other growing pains similarly reported on in forthright manner.

For those who are moving toward the development of a nongraded school, here is a living report of how one school handled the "Years of Changeover." Viewed from a present point of time, the logic of the movement, the critical need, and the modest early successes of some programs all combine to portend a rising tide of nongraded schools in the years ahead. Viewed from a subsequent point in time, the record will doubtless show that Dr. Dufay has made an important contribution to the cause of nongradedness during its formative years.

A Program For Ungrading

It is a startling truth: No two snowflakes are alike! But this fact regarding snowflakes is of small consequence to the destiny of our nation. Our greater concern must be for facts relating to a more complex group, infinitely more precious and more crucial to the future welfare of our society—our children. Common sense, as well as experience and intuition, tells us that children are indeed also in the no-two-are-alike category.

Unfortunately and paradoxically, common sense is not the common commodity implied by its name. Or perhaps it is more possessed than utilized. To illustrate this, we may point to the fact that, despite the apparent uniqueness of each child, American education over the years has been based firmly on the determination that school children ought to be alike. Pupils have been treated accordingly in the classroom. The resulting frustrations, the unnecessary tragedies have not yet ceased. In classroom after classroom, the creative powers of children continue to be encapsulated by production-line techniques of instruction. Developing personalities are still humiliated and deformed by unreasonable, impossible demands.

Happily, the outlook for education is brighter now than at any time in American history. Real and dramatic change is in progress.

Many observers have attributed our recent, several educational breakthroughs to the shockingly brilliant space achievements of the Soviet Union. These Russian accomplishments had devastating effects upon our national ego. The ensuing anxiety, it is claimed, brought focus and pressure upon education to such a degree as to prod it into motion for change.

Whatever the reasons, the fetters of tradition have been loosened sufficiently to permit escape. Communities with courageous leadership have been reaching out in search of better ways of inducing pupil learning. Others are studying the innovative activities with deep interest, wondering about the ultimate advantages of the newer patterns, questioning their adaptibility. Could they follow suit?

Within a relatively short period of time, a wide variety of innovations are on the verge of becoming the new "traditions." On the elementary school scene, the foremost of trends is the ungraded school. It has been described as "revolutionary," "exciting," "an educational dream," "an opportunity for profoundly influencing all levels of education." The number of proselytized schools is unusually high. Yet, for each school that has joined the ranks of those ungraded, there are many others that remain indecisive. Of those, a number may be said to be merely flirtatious; the remaining districts, with intentions more serious, are studiously paying court.

Professional counselors and best friends advise against prolonged courtship. Caution becomes calamity when the period of exploration is unduly extended. In effect, it is an attempt to carry on two quite different ways of life without a firm commitment to either. Conflict and confusion must result.

Giving impetus to the movement toward the ungraded school, there have been writings strongly favoring the notion. The most comprehensive of these has dealt quite adequately with a generally philosophical treatment. Yet, in all of the writings there has been little of spelled-out specifics. Thus, while many front-line educators are poised in readiness for the adventure that has been so extravagantly and glowingly portrayed, they are restrained by a natural reluctance to move forward in relative darkness. They may know *why*, but they wish, also, to know *how*.

This book has come into existence to accommodate those elementary school principals who are ready for the *how* step. While much of the material appears to be a reflection of my own ungraded program at Parkway School, the Parkway program itself stems from several years of study of other programs throughout the United States. It is based on solid experience, from procedures of implementation to the operation of program.

Pitfalls are clearly marked. Admittedly, there can be no one program for all schools. What is described is meant as a springboard, a point of departure. I would hope in this manner, to terminate a number of previously described courtships . . . in favor of the more honorable state of marriage. The ungraded school is a worthy life partner.

Contents

1

The Ungraded School: What Is It?

Those who would contemplate the values of the ungraded school ought to recognize the scope of their undertaking. In its purest form, the ungraded school—which is a philosophy—permeates every aspect of school program. In practice, however, we will find enough divergence to confound us, to make any investigator wonder about the apparent conflicts that come to light. Even the designation of the concept lacks standardization.

Some communities refer to their *ungraded primary plan;* others, having absorbed *all* of their elementary grades, call it *the ungraded school.* In some instances, the term *nongraded* is preferred. Another title used synonymously is: *the continuous progress plan.* There may be others.

Beyond the naming, there is need for definition. In the *Dictionary of Education* the ungraded primary school is described as "a school that has a flexible system of grouping in which the children in the primary grades are grouped together regardless of age and in which extensive effort is made to adapt instruction to individual differences."[1] My own interpretation, arising from investigation and experience, calls it *"a philosophy of education that includes the notion of continuous pupil progress, which promotes flexibility in grouping by the device of removing grade labels, which is designed to facilitate the teacher's role in providing for pupils' individual differences, and which is intended to eliminate or lessen the problems of retention and acceleration."*

Following the Second World War, communities in various parts of our nation initiated one form or another of the ungraded school. Before, there were but a few isolated communities that practiced the plan. The idea spread slowly at first. International crises, in successive waves, proved a boon to those who favor innovation and change. They are credited with beginning education's period of intensive movement toward change. The number of communities to begin some kind of ungrading multiplied rapidly.

Without a standardized procedure, and there is none, it is understandable that the ungraded program of District X is unlike the program of District A. Consider the aspect of grade labels eliminated. Some schools include kindergarten; most do not. Many restrict the ungrading to their primary units. Others have included the intermediate levels, up to what was previously grade eight. Table I (p. 26) demonstrates the variations in a sampling of the "pioneer" districts, those that undertook the challenge of organizational change prior to 1959. (It is to be expected that changes have been made in some of these communities since the study.)

Certain trends are revealed through Table I. Of the communities surveyed, only Corona, California, began its revised organizational scheme by replacing grades beyond the primary unit. It later returned grade four to the graded structure "for reasons of district growth." It is assumed that the schools involved at first housed

---

[1] Carter V. Good, *Dictionary of Education*. New York: McGraw-Hill Book Company, 1952, p. 586.

pupils up to grade four, and that increased enrollment at the lower levels pushed grade four out, leaving the buildings to care exclusively for primary children.

Eight of the thirty communities illustrated began their ungrading by replacing only the first grade in the first year of change. Gradually, grades two and three were also replaced by seven of the eight communities; in Cabool, Missouri, grades one through eight were replaced.

Perhaps the intent of the "gradualism versus abrupt change" approach was to enable participants to analyze their progress more carefully. Perhaps, also, it was used to lessen the anxieties that are known to accompany change, thereby serving to reduce resistance.

The differences in the naming of the concept and in the procedures of re-organization are of less consequence than the differences in interpretation. Investigation has found that some communities are quite content with having ungraded the reading program . . . and this may be, for them, the total extent of the ungrading process. To a lesser degree, school districts attempt ungrading of other subject areas.

To some, ungrading has meant *very* homogeneous grouping, coupled with some form of departmentalization. Others prefer less rigidly controlled forms of grouping and a continuation of the self-contained classroom. In another instance, it was felt that keeping one teacher with a group of children for their entire primary school experience was most desirable. This was described as a feature of the ungraded school.

How may we justify such variety under that single banner, the ungraded school? There is a single basic difference between the graded and the ungraded schools. In the truly graded school, the program is first established—according to grades—and children are expected to adapt to that existing program. That one program is geared to that mythical "average child." In the truly ungraded school, the ultimate objective is the tailoring of programs to the individual child, with adjustments made in the program. *Replacing*

TABLE I

ORGANIZATIONAL PATTERNS
AND SCOPE OF PARTICIPATION

Community	Year Initiated	Grades Replaced 1st year
Carona, Calif.	1951	1-4
Hawthorne, Calif.	1952	1-3
La Junta, Colo.	1947	1
Hillsborough Co., Tampa, Florida	1947	1-2
Athens, Georgia	1938	1-3
Douglas, Georgia	1950	1
Savannah, Georgia	1956	1
Maywood, Illinois	1949	1-3
Moline, Illinois	1956	1-3
Park Forest, Ill.	1950	1-3
Waukeegan, Ill.	1950	1-3
Gloucester, Mass.	1948	1-3
Marblehead, Mass.	1951	K-3
Dearborn, Mich.	1955	K-3
Grosse Pointe Woods, Mich.	1956	1-3
Warren, Mich.	1943	1-3
International Falls, Minn.	1947	1-3
Cabool, Missouri	1950	1
Hawthorne, Mo.	1947	1-3
Reno, Nevada	1952	1
Vestal, N. Y.	1958	K-1
Dayton, Ohio	1953	1-3
Youngstown, Ohio	1938	1-3
Cranston, R. I.	1951	1
Rock Hill, S. C.	1950	1-3
Burlington, Vt.	1952	1-2
Bellevue, Wash.	1957	1-3
Edmonds, Wash.	1955	1-3
Green Bay, Wisc.	1950	1
Milwaukee, Wisc.	1952	1

* returned to graded organization

Grades Now Replaced	Other Changes Anticipated	No. Elementary Schools		
		Participating 1st year	Now Participating	In District
1-3	No	4	11	11
1-4	No	1	1	8
1-3	No	1	1	7
1-3	N. R.***	40	70	70
1-6	No	1	2	8
1-3	Ext.**	1	12	12
1-3	No	1	42	42
K-8	No	10	10	10
1-3	No	1	4	20
1-3	No.	1	9	9
None*	New Study	1	0	18
1-6	No	2	10	10
K-3	No	5	7	7
K-3	No	25	25	25
1-6	No	1	1	10
1-3	N. R.***	1	5	5
1-3	Plus K	3	3	3
1-8	No	1	1	1
K-3	Ext.**	1	10	10
1-3	No	8	19	31
1-4	1-6	1	4	4
K-3	4-8	1	36	55
1-3	N. R.***	1	32	32
None*	No	2	0	19
1-3	4-6	1	1	1
K-3	N. R.***	1	2	10
1-3	No	2	7	16
K-6	No	1	3	16
1-3	Ext.**	2	14	14
1-3	No	1	114	116

** consideration of upward extension   *** no response

upward movement on a grade basis, the notion of continuous progress permits upward movement according to the real abilities of students. This movement is not dictated by previously set time sections, but by actual growth, whatever the pupil rate of learning.

Of course it is possibly true that graded schools exist (not truly graded) that are less grade-conscious and more individualized than some ungraded schools (not truly ungraded). Obviously the mere designation of a school as being ungraded . . . or graded . . . does not assure a program in harmony with that title. Every situation is a matter of degree. Are there *any* schools that are totally graded or ungraded?

A question arises: May we not develop a modern individualized program without resorting to the formal elimination of grade names? To a degree, yes—even to a large degree. But we must follow this question with a related one: Will the keeping of grade labels in some way serve the school in the attainment of its goals?

Practicing building administrators will find repeatedly that the existence of grade names serves as a frustrating hindrance, interfering with good common sense practice. To illustrate, let us assume that a school has been dedicated to the idea of serving the individual student, that—in most respects—the school is ungraded. Grade names, however, are tolerated. The school houses four first, four second, four third, four fourth, and four fifth grades.

In assigning pupils to classes, unless retention or acceleration is used, the placement is severely restricted. A child may be put into one of four classes. With the labels removed, the latitude permitted is considerably widened. We are able to place the moving child without specifying promotion, retention, or acceleration. There is no irrevocable commitment for we do not shackle ourselves to the meaningless phrases that frequently have served only to trap us. We may move a child out during the course of the year with the same freedom. Our larger selection of places (classes) insures each child a best possible "fit."

And what of the grade as an idea? Does not the third grade

teacher feel that those children in her care who are not at or above grade level are then below grade level—unsuccessful students? We may tell that teacher that *grade* is to be ignored, but if we insist that she is a third grade teacher we are making contradictory statements. Is this necessary? Does the same thing hold true for parents, i.e., do we advise them that grade name is of no consequence at the same time that we label their youngsters as students of particular grades? May we say the same for the students?

Perhaps the difference that is made, between labeling or not, is a subtle one. The distinction made may be appreciated only by *some* staff, *some* parents, and *some* children. I will contend that it is proper and desirable to make subtle improvements, and that subtlety itself is a hallmark of the true professional. Further, to tolerate the use of the grade label when it is in conflict with our beliefs is uncourageous. It is accommodating resistance to change, and sidestepping responsibilities.

Repeating the initial statement in this chapter, the ungraded school, in its purest form, permeates every aspect of school program. All subjects are ungraded. Specialists ungrade their specialties. Reports to parents reflect the philosophy, as do all records. Grade labels are removed.

Many, most, if not all of the ungraded schools are *partially* ungraded. Perhaps, with time and experience, with the development of new and more appropriate materials, with maturation and sophistication of staff, with revised curricula, with greater community support, all ungraded schools will become more so.

Research on how children best learn dramatically supports the philosophy of the ungraded school. Despite the unavoidable resistance of reactionary segments of community, a properly informed public will tend to support, appreciate, and even demand the better quality of education promoted by the new plan. The ungraded school must and will replace the graded one . . . throughout the nation.

SUPPORTERS OF THE CONCEPT

Despite the varied interpretations of the notion, there is mounting, almost massive agreement by well-regarded spokesmen that the philosophy inherent in the ungraded school is the philosophy of the future. Support comes from within and from without the profession. Following are some typical comments taken from interested magazines and newspapers:

> A revolution is taking place in the first three grades of many elementary schools . . . these elementary schools have taken a step (the nongraded plan) which may have more impact on the American educational system than all of the changes that are being contemplated in our high schools.[2]

> This is a dream, of course (the nongraded school). But it is being dreamed by educational administrators who have, in the past, often been caught dreaming about the preservation of the status quo . . . Their concern now is with real children.[3]

> The nongraded pattern of organization, together with the body of philosophical and psychological principles which give it meaning, has the opportunity for influencing profoundly the pattern and organization of elementary education in America and possibly secondary and higher education as well.[4]

In a speech given at a national convention of the School Boards Association, Gardner Cowles, Editor-In-Chief of *Look* Magazine, had these comments about ungrading, which were, in fact, recommendations for uplifting education in this country:

> . . . The ungraded approach has proved itself in school after school across the nation. You will find its flexibility especially valuable here.

---

[2] Editorial, "The Ungraded Primary," *School Management*, (November, 1959), p. 40.

[3] Fred M. Hechinger, "The Crystal Ball," *New York Times*, (March 25, 1962).

[4] Hugh V. Perkins, "Nongraded Programs: What Progress?" *Educational Leadership*, (December, 1961) p. 194.

Additional teachers will be assigned to these ungraded three years so that at crucial points—for example, the opening weeks of what is now kindergarten and the first weeks of reading—the teacher-pupil ratio may be reduced to ten-to-one.[5]

Stuart E. Dean, elementary school specialist for the United States Office of Education, denouncing graded organization as "blind to some of the important factors that govern and influence the instructional side of the school," spoke in favor of those measures which promote "continuous flexibility and fluidity . . . in nongradedness multi-gradedness, or some other flexible arrangement. If we believe in and are committed to a doctrine of individual differences—the range of human variability, then our methods of organizing the educational program must operate in support of this conviction." [6]

A statement endorsed jointly by the American Association of School Administrators and the National Education Association points out the conflict between the need to provide for the individual pupil and the graded plan of organization:

> Many present school practices need re-examination; and the assumptions underlying them and their effects, both good and bad, on the individual pupil, need careful scrutiny. Among these practices may be listed the following: Graded organization, although this plan of grouping children by the 'ladder' concept— changing one whole rung once a year—is almost a universal practice, the need for re-examination of the plan is obvious when it is viewed in the light of individual differences.[7]

The quality and the scope of support is impressive. The possibility of recantation is remote. The greater liklihood is a continuous swelling of the ranks of proponents.

---

[5] Excerpted from speech given by Gardner Cowles, Editor-in-Chief, *Look* Magazine, at 25th Annual Convention of the National School Boards Association at Boston, Mass., April 5, 1965.

[6] Elementary Principal's Letter, Vol. 5, No. 5, *Croft Educational Services*, (December, 1963), p. 1.

[7] *Labels and Fingerprints*. Washington, D. C.: National Education Association, 1960.

WHAT PROOF OF SUCCESS?

Those who would accept only research that meets the exacting standards of professional researchers may be shocked at finding a scarcity of data pertaining to the successes of the ungraded school, yet this has been the case. Most evaluations made have been overly subjective. The measures and the tools of measurement have not, in general, been precise. If, indeed, the concept of the ungraded school is more of a philosophy than it is a specific practice, how is a philosophy to be measured? It is plausible, or it is not. It is accepted, or not, by the individuals charged with implementing it. Attempting to apply standardized scoring to such an intangible appears to be a prosaic, unrewarding, even a futile endeavor.

What has been measured, sometimes quite casually, are results of a particular interpretation. Improved achievement in reading is most often reported. Certain communities have noted improvement in other areas, such as spelling, language usage, and arithmetic. Others have found that the practices of the ungraded school brought about improved personality adjustment in pupils. There have even been studies which demonstrated that pupils in graded schools have fared better than pupils in ungraded schools! These last are rare.

The studies may not be given as positive proof that the ungraded school produces all of the fine things attributed to it by its proponents. Nevertheless, it can be more easily assumed that those school districts that have incorporated some scheme of ungrading are pleased with the results they have obtained. They are staying with it; generally, they are expanding. Probably, with experience, they are modifying their practices. Definitely, they are committed to the philosophy they have endorsed.

Perhaps the overwhelming absence of substantiating evidence, unchallengable, ought not to provoke feelings of guilt or shame. Logic is firmly on the side of those of us who wish to accommodate the individual student, who believe that the differences among students are profound, who are thoroughly disenchanted with that Prussian heirloom, the grade, and who would rather eliminate it than constantly seek to circumvent its entrapments. Educational intuition, born of experience, also called insight, leads streams of educators, unrelentingly, to search out the ways of serving the children in their care in better ways . . . in the direction of the ungraded school or, better phrased, the pupil-programmed school. Whatever the name of excellence, the modern educator, unlike the reactionary of yesteryear, is action-prone, in dynamic pursuit of the loftier goals of his calling. Paper-proof is less important to him than the test of his own experience.

2

Grouping: The Vital Preliminary

"May we visit and see your ungraded elementary school in operation?" This is not an uncommon request. To a degree, we are able to show the visitor our ungraded school but, in most instances, what is seen simply raises more questions than are answered by observation. For that reason, all visitors are given a pre-visit talk by the principal. Following the visit, the observer gets an opportunity for a question-answer session.

The many behind-the-scenes operations, invisible during the time of classroom observation, are integral in their relatedness to the ungraded program. One such operation is the development of class groups. This ordinarily takes place near the end of a school year and in anticipation of the oncoming year.

When children are most appropriately assigned, and the make-up of the class group is most carefully developed, teachers ought to be most efficient and most effective. On the other hand, classes not well put together will limit the teachers' instructional efficiency.

Grouping has always been controversial, particularly among educational theorists. The classic struggle has been between the proponents of heterogeneous grouping and those preferring homogeneity. An emerging third party suggests that "you can group any old way you please." At this time, the last position seems hardly very helpful. Many districts have taken a middle course between the extremes of homogeneous and random heterogeneous planning.

The experienced, professional classroom teacher shows preference for a pupil distribution wherein each class has its share of pupil leaders, where the range of abilities is controlled, where the inevitable problems are equitably apportioned so as to reduce the probability of the class being predisposed to enervating chaos. Precision in following a grouping plan is largely controlled by number, i.e., the number of classes to be dealt with. Schools with the smallest number of classes could ordinarily expect the least degree of refinement in grouping.

Proper grouping requires that various other factors be considered, including teacher and even parent personalities. Whatever has a real effect on class make-up must be anticipated, searched for, and eventually acted upon. Final determination is made as a result of a set of values. Is it more important to avoid personality clash or to have even distribution of leadership? . . . ad infinitum.

The grouping aims, as defined, might well be met within the structure of the graded school. They are better met in the ungraded school, all other factors being equal.

GENERAL DESCRIPTION - THE PARKWAY SCHOOL

For purposes of illustration, the grouping procedures used at the Parkway School of Plainview, New York, are detailed in this chapter. The factors of school size or kinds of available staff may require some adjustments in relating the described grouping plan to other schools, but by no means should this present insurmountable obstacles. Moreover, it should hardly be considered necessary or even desirable to accept, in total, the specific procedures as outlined here. They are better thought of as guidelines.

Certain basic and general information about the Parkway School setting are presented in order to better appreciate the description of the grouping process.

Parkway is one of nine elementary schools in the district known as Central School District No. 4, a middle and upper-middle income community otherwise identified as Plainview-Old Bethpage of suburban Long Island, New York. Its enrollment of over 800 just previous to the final steps of ungrading made it the largest of the elementary schools in the district.[1]

The breakdown of pupil population, by grades, was as follows:

Kindergarten:	133	(6	classes)
Grade 1:	143	(6	”)
Grade 2:	125	(5	”)
Grade 3:	140	(5	”)
Grade 4:	133	(5	”)
Grade 5:	127	(5	”)

                      801

Full-time professional personnel other than the classroom teachers included: one art teacher, one librarian, one male physical education instructor, one vocal music teacher, one nurse-teacher, and one assistant principal.

Part-time professional personnel included: reading consultant (half-time), psychologist (half-time), female physical education teacher (half-time), speech teacher (one-third time), and an instrumental music teacher (about one-third time).

---

[1] "Final steps of ungrading" refers to the elimination of grade designations. Prior to that, the curriculum had been ungraded, as well as the instruction itself.

The absence of the sixth grade from the elementary set-up was due entirely to the pressure of an increasing pupil population at the lower levels; housing for the sixth grade in the junior high school building was simply a stop-gap measure.

Preparing for a New Organizational Pattern

The previously cited enrollment figures are those to be issued in the ensuing pages to depict the organizational transition from the graded to the ungraded structure. In Parkway's first year of formal changeover, there was an elimination of grade designations One, Two, and Three. It was the plan to eliminate grade labels annually until the elementary school was totally ungraded.

A breakdown of the over-all task would indicate these general requirements for grouping:

1. The identification of each kindergarten child's level of readiness for reading instruction.

2. The identification of these other factors which, if present, would influence grouping (kindergarten, grade I and II).

3. The identification of each pupil's reading instructional level (grades I and II).

4. The assignment of pupils to classes according to established criteria.

5. The assignment of teachers to classes.

Identifying the Kindergarten Child's Readiness

To identify the kindergartener's level of readiness for reading, a ranking system was used. In all instances, the youngster was considered ultimately to be at one of four levels, as defined:

Level 1: In need of more kindergarten-type experiences: these generally exclude formal readiness work, but would include those games and informal activities which are an integral part of readiness.

Level 2: In need of more formal readiness; readiness workbooks which are a part of a basal series may be
utilized.

Level 3: Children high in readiness; those children are ready
to begin formal reading after a brief introductory
period.

Level 4: Children able to read; those youngsters already have
had some experience in word identification and
sentence reading.

The above are satisfactory as broad categorizations. All assignments of "level" are made with the reservations that stem from an
appreciation of the difficulties of making "absolute" judgments. As
a concession to the possibility of error, particularly in the marginal
cases, there is the standing rule that changes be made as soon as
experience proves the error.

A "Kindergarten Check-Sheet For Reading Readiness" was employed as a device to aid in the catergorization process. A committee of kindergarten teachers and reading consultants developed a
list which included twelve items. These items were selected on the
basis of their ability to pinpoint degree of readiness to read. It
should be noted that this checklist had been used in the previous
school year and showed an unusually high degree of reliability.

In the sample check-sheet shown in the following illustration,
numbers 1, 2, 3, and 4 were used for each of the twelve items.
On the basis of the results of the twelve item check, an overall ranking was given. In all cases teacher judgment was the final determining factor in establishing rank. There were no absolute rules or
special formula adhered to.

As a further means of standardizing the ranking process, the
available reading consultant devoted several weeks near the end of
the school year in working with the children within the classroom.
As the "second teacher" within the room, the consultant was able
to develop a point of view that comes only from working *directly*

PARKWAY SCHOOL   KINDERGARTEN CHECK-SHEET FOR READING READINES

(X) A.M.   (_) P.M.   Teacher: **Mrs. Merrill**

NAME	OVERALL RANK 1 2 3 4	AUDITORY RHYMING	AUDITORY BEGINNING SOUNDS	VISUAL-GROSS SHAPES	VISUAL MATCHING WORDS & LETTERS	LETTER NAMES	SPEAKING VOCABULARY	LISTENING VOCABULARY (COMPREHENSION)	FOLLOWS DIRECTIONS	ATTENTION SPAN	RETENTION (MEMORY)	EYE-HAND COORDINATION	INTEREST IN LEARNING
Adams, Mary	1	1	1	2	2	1	2	1	1	1	2	2	1
Barnes, John	2	2	1	2	2	2	2	2	3	2	2	3	2
Baird, Fred	2	2	2	1	2	2	3	2	3	2	2	2	2
Beaumont, Ann	1	1	1	1	1	1	1	1	1	1	1	2	1
Desmond, Fred	3	3	3	3	3	4	3	4	3	3	2	3	3
Sommer, Sally	3	3	2	3	3	3	4	4	3	4	3	3	2

with the studied children. Finally, in individual meetings with each of the three teachers, each of the kindergarteners was ranked. Because of the consultant's involvement, there was less likelihood of there being sharp differences in teacher judgment among the kindergarten teachers.

A matter of interest to school administrators: the mere existence of the twelve items on the checklist served partially to define the kindergarten teacher's role in stimulating readiness. There was the realization of the district's specific expectations. Further, teachers were made aware that the kind of evaluation required was a throughout-the-year process rather than an end-of-the-year chore. An item by item examination of the checklist follows:

1. *Auditory Rhyming.* Has the child developed the ability to hear rhyming words, recognizing them as such: cat, rat, hat, mouse, house, blouse? If given four or five words, one not rhyming, is he able to pick out the one word that does not rhyme?

2. *Auditory Beginning Sounds.* Is the child able to select those words, which he hears, which begin with the same initial sound?

3. *Visual—Gross Shapes.* Is the child able to recognize the similarity and dissimilarity of the common shapes: triangles, squares, circles, etc.?

4. *Visual—Matching Words and Letters.* Is the child able to select the matching words or letters when he sees a small group of words or letters together? Illustration: *Sally . . . Sand Mary Sally Sorry.*

5. *Letter Names.* Is the child able to identify the letters of the alphabet in mixed order?

6. *Speaking Vocabulary.* How does the child compare with his peers or with his age group in this category?

7. *Listening Vocabulary (Comprehension).* After listening to a story, how well is the child able to interpret what he has heard?

8. *Follows Directions.* To what degree is the child able to follow oral directions, from the simplest to the more complex?

9. *Attention Span.* For how long a period is the child able to focus on an activity? How does he compare with his age group?

10. *Retention (Memory).* How does he rank with his age group in his ability to remember details of a story, memorization of a poem?

11. *Eye-Hand Coordination.* How well can he duplicate on paper figures that he sees on the chalkboard? Is he able to contain crayon marks within boundaries?

12. *Interest in Learning to Read.* This one item should reflect, generally, an overall ability in the preceding items as well as a willingness to cope with the printed symbol.

Identifying Other Factors in Grouping

The next step in the grouping process was the filling out of the Pupil Profile Cards for each youngster. This was done not only in kindergarten, but in grades I and II.

PUPIL PROFILE CARD

DATE _____

NAME OF CHILD _____ GRADE _____

SEX: M ___ F ___   TEACHER _____

READING INSTRUCTIONAL LEVEL:
    CRITERIA: _____

Check Appropriate Areas:

    Outstanding Social Characteristics:
        Teacher Evaluation: Leader ( )   Isolate ( )

* Emotional Needs Which Warrant Special Placement ( )
* Health Problems Which Warrant Special Placement ( )
* Speech Problems Which Warrant Special Placement ( )
* Other Problems Which Warrant Special Placement   ( )

Class Placement, September, 19_____
* Factors considered should be entered in Cumulative Record
  Folder

The Pupil Profile Card, as illustrated, is printed on a regulation 5" x 8" index card. For easier identification, the cards are printed in various colors, each representing a different level. Blue was used for the kindergarten teacher, pink by first grade teachers, yellow by

second grade teachers, orange by third grade teachers, etc. In ensuing years, the colors would represent the number of years the
pupil has been in school. Additionally, the right hand corner of the
girls' cards are clipped, for convenient handling.

In response to the item, *Reading Instructional Level,* the kindergarten teacher would indicate Level 1, 2, 3, or 4, as previously defined. Next to *Criteria* she would note: Reading Readiness Check-
sheet.

In determining whether to check any of the other items, as factors in placement, the teacher is expected to use her own judgment,
primarily, on the basis of her daily experiences with each of her
charges. However, there are definite aids available in the form of
lists of characteristics for each of the categories. Under *leadership,*
for example, are items such as: *is looked to by others when something must be decided; can take charge of a group; is able to influence others to work toward desirable goals, etc.* These lists may be
established by the professional group, themselves, or may be found
in guidance handbooks, such as, *Identifying Children With Special
Needs.* [2]

If the profile cards are to serve their intended purpose, every
effort must be made by the building administration to reasonably
standardize teacher interpretation of what is "an emotional problem," a "leader," etc. The lists are one means of doing this. Equally
important, however, are meetings where building administration
and teaching staff discuss the use of the profile card, its intended
function, the need for standardization. Moreover, minutes of the
meeting should be dittoed and distributed for use as reference.

Teachers should be encouraged to treat the cards in the fashion
of worksheets, writing in whatever additional information may appear useful. This is of particular help when a check is placed against
"other problems."

---

[2] Jack Kough and Robert F. DeHaan, *Identifying Children with Special
Needs,* Science Research Associates, Incorporated, 1955.

TEACHER'S CLASS PROFILE SHEET*

Teacher: Mrs. Parkell   Room 3   B:11 + G:13 = T:24

NAME	READING	LEADER	ISOLATE	EMOTIONAL	HEALTH	SPEECH	OTHER
Arnold, Frank	Level 1			X		X	
Cramer, Bruce	3						
Donnelly, John	2		X		X	X	
Gurwitz, Irving	2					X	
Morse, Fred	3	X					
Barnes, Eva	4	X					
Caroll, Joan	2			X			X
Lester, Ann	4						
TOTALS	X	2	1	2	1	3	1

*this is a fictitious class, of course; a total of 24 names were not entered simply to conserve space.

44

Upon completion of the profile cards a "Teacher's Class Profile Sheet" should be made up, as in the sample on page 44.

After the building principal receives all of the kindergarten teachers' class profile sheets, he would be able to put together the composite grade grouping sheet, as illustrated below.

COMPOSITE GRADE GROUPING SHEET

NAME OF SCHOOL: PARKWAY
PRESENT GRADE: Kindergarten

READING

Level	1	2	3	4			
Totals	24	35	37	35			

SOCIAL CHARACTERISTICS

Leadership	16
Isolates	5

DISTRIBUTION OF EXCEPTIONAL CHILDREN

Speech	9
Health	5
Emotional	5
Other	2

Boys 71   Girls 62   Total 133

The class profile sheets and the composite grade grouping sheets illustrated were utilized for all classes being ungraded, including Kindergarten, grades I and II.

IDENTIFYING READING INSTRUCTIONAL LEVEL (GRADES I AND II)

Levels 1, 2, 3, and 4 have already been defined. After obtaining all information about the reading levels of the children who would be part of the ungraded structure, it was seen that we would be working with a range of reading abilities that extended to Level 12, according to the following redefinition of terms:

Primer	Level 5
1^2 low	6
1^2 high	7
2^1 low	8
2^1 high	9
2^2 low	10
2^2 high	11
3^1	12

While it may not be common practice to differentiate between a *high* and a *low*, as above, the classroom teachers insisted that there was a real enough difference between one reading series and another to justify this demarcation. This has been substantiated by an analysis of content of each of the reading series (we actually employ three series which we refer to as our basics and others which are described as our supplementary).

In listing each child's instructional level on the individual profile cards, it was decided to indicate the specific level being completed at the time the cards were being made out. We could just as well have written the anticipated level for the beginning of the oncoming school year.

The designation of *instructional level* raises a problem which also provokes some teacher uneasiness. After a teacher operates with a class for a period of time at the beginning of a school year, it is not unusual for her to discover that she could possibly have five or six reading groups. No one, in setting up the class, intended it to be that way; but despite good intentions, it happens. To further complicate matters, it is fairly usual, in the suburbias of Long Island, to have new entrants pop up during all parts of the school year.

To accommodate the problem as well as to avoid the inefficiency that might otherwise result, the classroom teacher engages in the practice of "shoehorning" that is, placing a child with a reading group which is not the best possible in terms of the child's real ability, but which is the best possible in terms of the groupings that exist in that classroom.

At the end of the school year, then, when children's instructional levels are being indicated on the profile cards, teachers are faced with a quandary: whether to list the level at which the child has been operating, or to list the studied estimate of real ability? The answer is obvious enough, but teachers must be made aware of administration's appreciation of the problem; the discomfiture of the guilt feeling is real and should be avoided.

There is no need to easily accept the problem of "shoehorning." This will remain a problem, of course, when the *actual* instructional level is not shown by an embarrassed teacher. It will remain, also, if no provision is made during the course of the year for regrouping.

Plainview has had a policy *on the books* which would allow changes in placement within the first six weeks of school. It was rare for anyone to take full advantage of the opportunity to make changes. . . .for reasons that the front-line educators know too well. The movement of a child, after school has been in operation for a while, stirs up parental anxiety to a surprising degree. To avoid undue unpleasantness, the teachers involved in the change, and the building administration, must employ a number of public-relations tools including: the don't-be-alarmed-this-is-a-normal-procedure letter; and the personal conference with the sending teacher, the receiving teacher, and the principal. After these procedures are used there is always the feeling the parent has not been convinced. It can very well be unpleasant. Add to this the clerical trivia that is required: the changes in register, the cumulative records, the central office involvement (they must be notified and the move justified), and we can now better appreciate the reluctance to use the policy.

This intrepid administrator and his intrepid first grade staff did test the results of relatively large scale changes in placement. After the first six weeks of one school year, fifteen such changes were made. The children were made ready, the letters went out. . .and we waited for the explosions.

Phones rang. Conferences were held. There were indeed parental expressions of concern, anger, and annoyance, as anticipated. Nor were all conclusions reached in sweet harmony.

Yet, at year's end, the decisions made proved proper. . .and this became our mode of operation. Further, it was our decision to make changes at any time during the course of the school year when such changes proved in the best interests of the youngsters.

The problem of making changes in placement after the start of a school year, while not large and overwhelming, is significant and definitely has effect on attempts to follow any plan of grouping.

ASSIGNING PUPILS TO CLASSES

The Principal's Paper Plan

Having in his possession the composite grade grouping sheets for the kindergarten, first, and second grades, the principal is able to develop a paper plan of grouping. This preliminary plan would show possible class groupings, perhaps more than one set, and would serve as a jumping-off point for discussion by staff. Only with full staff would the final grouping plan be put into existence. The principal would not need, initially, to delve into factors other than reading levels.

Taking the actual information gleaned from the grouping sheets, this was the make-up of the first nongraded group, in terms of reading levels:

Level 1 - 24;	Level 2 - 38;	Level 3 - 37;	Level 4 - 35;
Level 5 - 54;	Level 6 - 63;	Level 7 - 35;	Level 8 - 6;
Level 9 - 18;	Level 10 - 29;	Level 11 - 42;	Level 12 - 20.

The task was to distribute these children among the sixteen primary teachers, limiting the possible number of reading groups to three without resorting to an attempt at homogeneous grouping and the pitfalls therein. Further, those primary teachers with the children at the lowest levels would have to be given the classes of smallest enrollment. It has been conceded that it is difficult to provide programs of individualization where enrollment is high and particularly where the children have only minimum of skills (if any) which would otherwise permit a greater amount of near-independent study.

If possible, groups within a class would be contiguous, to enable movement within a class without "shoehorning," and without having to resort frequently to changes in class.

With the combination of the joy and seriousness that are the companions of new freedom, the principal was able to develop his plan within the acceptable and desirable framework but without the restrictions imposed those many years by the anachronistic grade barriers. This would lead to some interage mixing, of course, but the degree of this could be controlled. The decision was to limit the mixing to about four classes in the first year of operation, to develop some beginning experience.

A first paper plan was developed. It was informally shown to a few staff members for their reactions and then, with the help of the reading consultant, some revisions were made. The resulting second plan is illustrated on page 50.

It may be seen that in a number of cases, in the lower levels, the proposed classes were limited to two groupings. Experience has established the fact that after a few weeks of operation these classes would probably have a minimum of three working groups. Two other groups, H and I, were also limited to two groupings. In both instances there was the likelihood of inter-mixing second and third year primary pupils. By narrowing the range somewhat in these classes, we were attempting to better control the problems of classroom organization that would be a part of an age-mixed class.

Classes C, F, and G would probably contain first and second

PRINCIPAL'S PAPER PLAN
for
THE PRIMARY SCHOOL, THE PARKWAY SCHOOL

CLASS	1	2	3	4	5	6	7	8	9	10	11	12	TOTAL
A	8	13											21
B	8	13											21
*C	8	12											20
D			12	12									24
E			16	8									24
*F			9	7		8							24
*G				8	9	9							26
*H					16	9							25
*I					13	12							25
J					7	8	12						27
K					9	9	10						28
L						8	13	6					27
M									9	9	9		27
N									9	9	9		27
O										5	12	10	27
P										6	12	10	28
TOTALS	24	38	37	35	54	63	35	6	18	29	42	20	401

* Indicates inter-age mixing.

year primary students. Class C would have the three youngsters, immature, who would undoubtedly have been retained under the graded plan. While there is the strong possibility that they will remain an additional year in the elementary school, there are several years more before this decision will have to be rendered. Even then, it would be under the plan of continuous progress, without the stigma of retention and without the boredoms of repetition.

The second year primary students of classes F and G would not contain children who would otherwise have been retained. These children, average or somewhat better in overall performance, would have new social and academic roles.

With one exception we achieved contiguous grouping in our

classes. In that one class, Class F, it was decided that we would sacrifice contiguous grouping in order to place *at least* average (or better than) second year primary students with a preponderance of above-average first year primary pupils.

Comparing the class size under the paper plan of the nongraded primary with the class sizes that would have been necessary under the graded plan we may note:

Nongraded Plan	*Graded Plan*
By simple adjustments, we were able to control sizes so that all but two were 27 or less and so that the classes having the lower levels were those of smallest enrollment.	Average size of first grade classes: 22 Average size of second grade classes: 28.6 (this would have meant at least three classes of 29. With 6 or 7 probable retentions, there would have been instead 5 classes of 30) Average size of third grade classes: 24 or 25

Retention

It has been indicated that some ten children would have had to suffer retention under the graded plan. To the parents and even to the children involved it would have meant humiliation and repetition, repeating a grade, a waste of one year's time. For the teachers who would have had the retained children in their classes, it would have been difficult not to think of them as the "failures" who were placed with them, a sort of extra burden.

For the principal, it would have meant an enormous expenditure of time. Each recommendation for retention means that the principal must personally investigate each of the factors that are related: the child's real ability, his attitude, his social characteristics, etc. In most cases the psychologist reviews the child's profile with the principal and makes his recommendations, also. In those instances where it is decided that retention is indeed in the child's best interests, there are then the tear-filled conferences with the parents, frequently more than one for each case.

Throughout the history of public education in our country the problems of retention have held the attention of the decision-makers. Policy on promotion has run the gamut. There has been promotion, or no promotion, or double promotion ("skipping") based on absolute standards. Promotion has been annual, semi-annual, and quarterly.

Social promotion, described disparagingly as promotion without regard for accomplishment, is based largely on the desire not to injure children socially or psychologically. This "solution" has been criticized severely and generally has been modified. At the present time, the middle-of-the-road policy for many of the graded schools is to give consideration to the possible social and psychological effects that retention might have on the individual child; decisions are rendered only after a thorough exploration, oftentimes including the factor of parental reaction.

As a result of an awakening and sensitivity to the potential harm of ill-considered retentions, the practice of nonpromotion has been decreasing nationally, from a rate of 16% in 1909, to a failure rate of 8.3% in 1957. Nevertheless, the lesser rate still represents annual nonpromotion of millions of elementary school pupils. Thus it remains a major problem, its limitations and frustrations emphasized by reported research which says:

> Children who are not promoted do no better than children of like ability who are promoted. Nonpromotion practices do not reduce the range of specific abilities with which the teacher has to cope. The threat of nonpromotion does not cause threatened children to achieve more than those who are not threatened. The failing child is more likely to quit school, to be in difficulty with school authorities, to be antagonistic. The nonpromoted child has greater difficulty in making adjustments than the promoted child of the same ability.[3]

---

[3] Virgil E. Herrick, "Recent Criticisms of the Elementary School," *Encyclopedia of Educational Research*, ed. Chester W. Harris, (1960 Edition). New York: Macmillan Company, pp. 438-39.

Having rejected the assembly-line approach that created graded organization which, in turn, generated the befuddlements of promotion policy, our focus must turn to the proffered remedy of our nongraded school. Does a properly implemented program of continuous progress eliminate the vexations of the promotion rituals?

No district has outrightly claimed this distinction. However, there are those who would say yes, with explanation. It must still happen that children will be required to spend an additional year in a nongraded school and, in rarer instances, they may spend a year less. Yet, it will not be conceded that this is retention or acceleration.

The logic is apparent. If there are no grades (and none is identified in the nongraded unit), and if children progress continuously according to their individual abilities, and if the teacher makes genuine provision for the individual differences of children in terms of classroom program, it can be expected there will be a natural range of academic accomplishment. The range would be the result of differences in *rate of learning*, as well as because of native abilities, teacher-pupil relationships, home and outside environment, etc. Within a nongraded unit, provided that the curriculum and its objectives have been clearly established, it is conceivable that some children would achieve reasonable mastery in less than the accepted average time, while others would require additional time. In the accepted sense, the child who remained an additional year in a nongraded unit would not have suffered retention since he was not obliged to repeat a particular grade and all the content of that grade. Neal Neff, principal of a nongraded school in Cabool, Missouri, was explicit in his defense of the continuous progress concept: "We retain no children. If a child is going to be taught on his level, according to ability, wherever he is, how could one retain a child?"

It must be granted that promotion problems do not disappear upon the emergence of the nongraded plan. There is, however, a real and important distinction between the retention of the graded school and the "extended opportunity" offered by the nongraded school. But the difference is relatively subtle, sometimes fogged by the reluctant hard-core worshippers of the good old days.

Whatever the interpretation, experience tells us that there are fewer numbers of pupils given an additional year in the nongraded set-up than in the graded plan.

FINALIZATION OF GROUPING

The Principal's Paper Plan was done almost entirely with numbers, with no consideration given the factors other than reading. It was the task of the involved professional staff to deal with flesh-and-blood children as represented by the pupil profile cards and to come up with class groupings that would meet the set criteria.

The professional staff involved included: the sending teachers, the receiving teachers, the principal and the assistant principal, the reading consultant, the psychologist and, in some instances, the nurse. At each of the meetings held the materials required are: a chalkboard having on it a duplication of the paper plan, the pupil profile cards, the composite grade grouping sheets, and plenty of paper for scratch work.

There are any number of ways the meetings could have been organized. In most instances, either the principal or the assistant directed the activities; there was plenty of allowance for group interaction. Only the first and last meetings were with the full staff; there were many smaller group meetings. It was felt that the larger group would lose working efficiency, would limit participation too easily, and would bog down frequently.

At the first meeting, it was the purpose of the principal to orient the staff: to review the results of the grouping sheets, to give a description of the paper plan—how it was arrived at and what its purpose was, to outline the procedures that would be followed in developing the class lists. The staff was able to make comment, to ask questions, and to generally make preparation for the smaller meetings.

The first of the smaller meetings was held around the conference table in the principal's office. At the table were the three kindergarten teachers, the reading consultant, and the first grade teachers. The principal, using the portable chalkboard, directed the proceedings. Most of the activity, the card counting, trading, grouping, etc., was performed by the kindergarten teachers and the reading consultant. The first grade teachers functioned primarily as observers, although they were given opportunity to raise questions or to make comments.

To the extent possible we were going to follow the paper plan. As problems arose, if changes seemed desirable, then adjustments would be made. It was clearly understood that the best argument, in favor of the overall good, would win the decision.

The first task then was to develop one class, specifically Class A, having eight children on Level 1 and thirteen children on Level 2. To the extent possible, we would take large groups of children from one class, avoiding the situation wherein a child would be the single one from a particular class. We would, of course, take the opportunity to break up combinations of children which had resulted in social friction. Further, we would attempt to properly distribute the leadership, emotional problems, and those other factors described on the profile cards. Even distribution of boys and girls was necessarily a factor.

Following are some of the typical comments made at the meeting:

"There aren't enough 'sparks' in that class. Let's substitute Marion for Eva, and John for Edward."

"Putting Robert and Henry in the same class is dangerous; let's switch."

"We're overloaded with speech problems in this one class; let me have one Level 2 boy and one Level 3 girl without a speech problem."

The cards flew back and forth in that manner. When it began to look as though we would run out of reasons for altering a class make-up, we would stop, put a labeling band around our group of cards, and then proceed to put together a new class. And then another.

After putting together some five or six classes, provided the time did not run out, the group would then one by one, each teacher separately, review the make-up of the proposed classes. If any combination failed to suit them in this re-screening, they would write a comment on a piece of paper; they would then do the same for each proposed class.

Again, there would be some trading, each switch being fully justifiable to the group. There were, in fact, some minor adjustments to the paper plan as a result.

Obviously enough, the sending teachers bore the greatest responsibility for the make-up of the new classes. They knew most about the children being sent. The receiving teachers asked questions, served as overseers, insuring themselves that no class was composed expeditiously to their disadvantage. The reading consultant, aware of the overall reading program, acted as the resource person, commenting, helping, as needed. The principal's main function after the development of the paper plan, was to direct the activities and to see that the results of the groupings did not violate the spirit of the overall plan.

There had to be many small meetings and there were. There were countless numbers of informal discussions among staff. In addition to finally putting together the classes for the following year, teachers were getting and sharing information about the children.

The Nongraded Grouping Summary Sheet on pages 58 and 59 gives the final breakdown for the nongraded classes.

ASSIGNMENT OF TEACHERS

It was vitally important that the four teachers assigned the interage classes have some minimum qualifications. They should have had experience on more than one level *or,* in their teaching, have shown marked ability to provide an individualized program. . . which would, in fact, have been teaching on more than one level. Moreover, the provision for individual abilities should have been in areas in addition to reading. Additionally, the attitude of the teachers (regarding the prospect of having the interage classes) should have been one of genuine enthusiasm for the project.

Another minimum attribute of the teachers would be their ability to verbalize their experiences, to provide staff and all concerned parties with accurate reports of significant experiences. Obviously, this would be of greatest importance in the first year of operation, when the entire program would be subjected to closest scrutiny.

Insofar as assignment of the other twelve teachers, this had to be on the basis of knowledge of their abilities and experiences. How tempting was the idea of major re-shuffling, so that teachers for- merely identified with a particular grade would have, instead, tot- ally different age groups! This would have been a step in the right direction, but there would have been some real sacrifices required. My first-year primary teachers had proved an extraordinary combi- nation who worked beautifully together and who thrived on the challenges presented by the first year primary students. To switch any of the other primary teachers to this assignment would seem a relatively frivolous gesture. The decision was to keep people with the age group with which they were most comfortable, for that first year of operation. We would proceed slowly, risk less, and probably accomplish more.

The assignment of teachers to classes having been made, we had completed the final step of the process. Insofar as grouping was concerned, we were ready for the coming year.

SUMMARY

One aspect of the nongraded school, unseen but vital, is the group- ing of children for classroom assignment. It is contended that the

PART I

NONGRADED GROUPING SUMMARY SHEET PARKWAY SCHOOL

Reading Level	Class A B	Class A G	Class B B	Class B G	Class C B	Class C G	Class D B	Class D G	Class E B	Class E G	Class F B	Class F G	Class G B	Class G G	Class H B	Class H G
1	6	2	6	2	5	3										
2	6	7	6	7	7	5										
3							8	4	8	8	5	4				
4							3	9	3	5	3	4	4	4		
5													4	5	12	4
6											5	4	4	5	4	5
TOTALS	12 + 9 = 21		12 + 9 = 21		12 + 8 = 20		11 + 13 = 24		11 + 13 = 24		13 + 12 = 25		12 + 14 = 26		16 + 9 = 25	
Leadership	2		2		2		3		3		3		2		3	
Isolates	0		1		0		0		1		1		0		1	
Speech	2		2		1		2		1		2		3		3	
Other Health	0		0		1		0		2		0		1		0	
Emotional	2		1		2		3		2		1		0		2	
Special Placement	1		0		0		0		1		0		1		0	

PART II NONGRADED GROUPING SUMMARY SHEET PARKWAY SCHOOL

Reading Level	Class I B	Class I G	Class J B	Class J G	Class K B	Class K G	Class L B	Class L G	Class M B	Class M G	Class N B	Class N G	Class O B	Class O G	Class P B	Class P G
5	6	7	5	2	6	3										
6	6	6	4	4	4	4	6	2								
7			4	8	3	7	3	10								
8							3	3								
9									5	4	4	5				
10									5	4	6	3	2	3	4	2
11									5	3	5	4	7	5	5	7
12													5	5	4	6
TOTALS	12 + 13 = 25		13 + 14 = 27		13 + 14 = 27		12 + 15 = 27		15 + 12 = 27		15 + 12 = 27		14 + 13 = 27		13 + 15 = 28	
Leadership	2		3		2		3		3		2		3		3	
Isolates	0		1		0		0		1		0		0		1	
Speech	2		3		0		2		2		0		2		0	
Other Health	1		0		0		0		0		1		0		0	
Emotional	2		3		1		2		2		1		2		1	
Special Placement	1		0		0		1		1		0		0		0	

class make-up has a definite effect on the potentials of the class-room instructional program. In organizing classes, efforts must be made: (1) to control the reading range; (2) to equitably distribute pupil leadership; and (3) to distribute the various social and health problems. Pupil assignment is accomplished without regard for age level or grade label, but entirely upon the basis of the other criteria established.

A first step to take in determining the best kind of grouping is accomplished through the use of a Kindergarten Check-Sheet For Reading Readiness. The reading consultant's direct involvement in interpreting the check-sheet served as another means of standardizing teacher judgment. The defining of the reading level of the other primary children is based on the teacher's judgment of their instructional level at the end of the school year. Children working in less-than-appropriate reading groups should be given designations based on their real ability.

All pertinent information is put on Pupil Profile Cards for all of the children. Each teacher develops a Class Profile Sheet which gives summary information on the class as a whole. From these the building principal is able to develop Composite Grade Grouping Sheets. The totals of these permit the creation of the Principal's Paper Plan, a possible pupil distribution based solely on indicated reading levels.

Finally, the staff involved, using the paper plan as a point of departure, begins the task of developing classes. Many meetings are required, large group, small group, formal, and informal. Every proposed class is subjected to countless refinements and modifications in order to meet the few but important criteria established.

Of the classes to be developed, some will have inter-age groupings, others will not. The number of age-mixed classes is controllable.

The immediate benefits of the nongraded grouping include:
(1) elimination or at least a lessening of the retention problems;

(2) greater control of class sizes; (3) greater control of reading ability range within the framework of the grouping criteria.

The assignment of teachers to each class is based, in all cases, on each teacher's background, and special abilities. Those who are to teach the age-mixed groups should be selected particularly for their positive attitudes, their skills at individualization of instruction, and their ability to communicate clearly their experiences. All teacher assignments should be based on their interests, abilities, and experiences.

3

Within the Ungraded Classrooms

On that first day of school early in September, in the Year of Changeover[1], over 800 youthful, polished faces reflected the high emotions that are a part of every first school day. Dozens of parents milled about, perhaps indulging their own tendencies to participate in the day's excitement. Teachers smiled broadly, holding up the placards which identified their room numbers, youngsters lined up dutifully before them. As with every school year, the air was charged with anticipation.

When the bell sounded, as the children poured through the school doors, it signaled the beginning of something new and special in the Parkway School. In sixteen of the thirty-two classrooms there would be no grade designations. Teachers and their children knew that there was to be but one descriptive term for each of

---

[1] The Year of Changeover is the first year that grade designations were officially eliminated.

those sixteen rooms: they were primarily classrooms. The teachers were primary teachers, and the children were primary pupils.

In four of the classrooms, despite the preparations that had been made, some of the children expressed varying degrees of shock and misgivings as they noted the presence of other children of a different age level. Some questions were ingenuously blunt, as, "Mrs. Merrill, did I get left back?" Mrs. Merrill was reassuring, as were the other teachers of the inter-age classes, but it became immediately apparent that words alone would not dispel the obvious concerns. There was some unlearning that would have to be accomplished through proper experiences.

Nor was the building principal spared the need to give words of explanation to parents anxious to shield their young ones from the unknown horrors of this strange new grouping plan. During those first few days many requests were made for conferences with the principal. In every case the explanations were on a one-to-one basis; it was a reiteration of what had been said at the large group meetings, in principal-to-parent letters, in small group meetings, in the many informal meetings that came about casually in school corridors during the day, or in the evenings at the various school functions.

> "Mrs. Blank, in our grouping this year we have placed children on the basis of factors other than age or previous grade. Each of our primary teachers has no more than three clearly-defined reading groups; each class has a core of pupil leadership; and the various physical, emotional, and social problems are distributed throughout the many classes. The purposes of our grouping in this way are to enable our staff to more efficiently instruct all the children, and to give the teachers greater opportunity for providing individualized instruction. I am absolutely confident that your child will profit from this arrangement, etc. . . ."

Parents *apparently* accepted the explanation. It was more probable that they adopted a wait-and-see attitude. Neither principal nor teachers needed to be told that only success would satisfy the questioning public.

It needs to be pointed out that, in the eyes of the principal, at least, "success" included but had to go beyond the narrower view of improved academic achievement.

REDUCING TEACHER PRESSURES

One of the best reasons for the discontinuance of the grade label is to relieve the pressures on the classroom teacher. Are not first grade teachers very much under the impression that they must prepare those first year students for second grade? When they are "unsuccessful" with some, aren't they letting down the second grade teachers, and the anxious parents of their slower-moving children, and the building administration (who evaluates them)? And perhaps the children?

Are not the "failures" made more prominent by the fact that the next-door teacher has no such failures. These are formidable pressures, indeed. Add to this the fact that the achievement test scores are usually translated into grade-level equivalents and posted conspicuously next to the teacher's name, a teacher of a particular grade. These pressures exist, of course, for all grade teachers.

Can grade teachers, the best of them, be criticized for ignoring or circumventing the realities of their classroom situations? It has happened that small children, unready for their primers, have been subjected to the rigors of those primers, and the resulting failures, despite the awareness of the teacher that this was the likely outcome. Unwise, expedient decisions of this sort are sired by the anxieties of the pressured teacher. The skipped steps weaken the essential bases of learning for the pushed-along children. With accumulation of failure, the pupil's responsiveness to learning declines.

To a lesser extent, the converse is also true. Children are prevented from handling material at a higher level than the grade number, despite the fact that this might well be at their real instructional level. There is a reluctance to "cause problems" for teachers of ensuing grades. To alleviate conscience, the word "enrichment" is used to describe an action which is, in essence, giving children "a lot more of the same." Children unchallenged and bored to begin with, could become *very* bored with *that* style of enrichment.

Plainly, we are dealing here with vital matters: the mental attitudes of teachers and pupils. When teachers, out of need, are forced to deal in an expedient manner with children (as with inappropriate shoehorn style placement), they may experience some unpleasant emotions—anger, annoyance with circumstances, even guilt. Conversely, in eliminating this kind of situation, positive effects on teachers' mental dispositions may be expected.

And what of the children? If success does breed success, then failure probably tends to produce more failure. The mental health of the slow-learning pupil for whom successful experiences are not provided suffers double jeopardy: initially, his own slowness, and then, the unpleasant consequences which beget the bitter fruits of failure and become a way of life. The faster children for whom no satisfying provisions are made, must tolerate the anguish of intellectual containment.

The prescription:

Take away the grade designations. Let building administration demonstrate a greater awareness of the ability groups within each of the classrooms, express encouragement to teachers to teach in honest regard of the realities of their classroom situations. Painstakingly, and frequently, advise parents of the advantages for their children in an ungraded program. Translate achievement scores into percentiles. In essence, reduce those pressures.

Hopefully, teachers may then begin to teach children, rather than children of a grade. Their expectations will stem from an understanding of the individual children, their real needs.

Was this the experience in Parkway School?

In the previous chapter the grouping make-up of ungraded classes previous to the opening of school was illustrated. Refinements were made in the beginning of the year. With groups clearly defined, the new emphasis (on realistic expectations) understood and accepted, teachers took on their assignments. After the first three months there were a number of groups of children that had not yet begun their pre-primers. At the other end of the scale, there were youngsters completing the advanced 3^2 series. In this short period, it was apparent that the idea was being put to the test. By year's end, some children in the primary groups were *successfully* completing their fundamental 1^1s and others the advanced 4^2s. This was not in accord with the *grade* plan, but it made sense.

CONTINUOUS PROGRESS IN READING

The development of reading skills is the foremost objective of the primary school—and rightfully so. A successful program of reading can be expected to foster pupil success in other subject areas.

The ungraded school calls for a reading plan based on the notion of continuous progress. In such a plan the pupil moves forward only as rapidly as his ability allows. His assignment to a group is the result of the teacher's identification of his true *instructional level*, the level at which the child is able to read with enough ease as to provide enjoyment, but with sufficient difficulty so that elements can be pulled out for instructional purposes.

When reading groups are carefully formed, with each pupil comfortably placed within the most appropriate group, the teacher may be expected to make maximum progress with the groups assigned to him. With grade designations no longer serving to influence and impede, the bounds are set by the abilities of the students themselves.

In some situations individual students—even after proper placement—by reason of *unusually* slow or rapid development within a group, will break the rhythm of the group and will need to be pulled from it. When possible, these students will simply be transferred to another group within the class. Having contiguous levels assigned to the teacher make this more possible. In any event, if we are not to violate the spirit of continuous progress, all steps essential to maintaining best placement must be taken.

EARLY YEAR ADJUSTMENTS IN PUPIL PLACEMENT

With the beginning of a new school year, the receiving teachers will find their pupils at the levels of reading indicated on the Pupil Profile Cards that are passed along with the pupils . . . in most instances. When there is doubt that lingers about any pupil's real instructional level, then a set procedure is followed for correction of placement. Ordinarily, the teacher waits a few weeks before initiating the procedure, verifying her suspicions with experience. It would apply, of course, only to those pupils who could not be placed elsewhere within the same class.

The reading consultant is informed, in writing, of all suspected misplacements. All referred pupils are tested by the consultant through the use of the Informal Reading Inventory. The results of the test are made known to the referring teacher. In nearly all instances the tests bear out the teacher's allegations; however, the inventory additionally serves to accurately pinpoint instructional level, facilitating new placement. In rare instances where teacher and consultant are in disagreement about the consultant's findings, the building principal makes the final determination. It is important that the classroom teacher not feel required to accept the consultant's findings. The greatest contribution of a consultant is in the role of resource person as opposed to authority figure. Additionally, the teacher acts as a check against the possible errors of the consultant.

After agreement is reached on the real instructional levels of the pupils to be transferred, the principal reviews the assigned levels of each primary teacher, and the numbers of children in each group. Since there is considerable overlapping—that is, since it is probable that there are two or more teachers handling each of the various reading levels—there is opportunity for placement on factors in addition to reading level. Once again, to the extent possible, consideration is given the factors of leadership and the physical, emotional, and social problems of the children being placed. Not bound by grade designation, we are able to make placement in any of the ungraded rooms.

In practice, the principal would decide changes in placement cooperatively with the reading consultant, the sending teachers, and the receiving teachers. Initial informal contacts would lead to a meeting of the staff involved and the principal. By subjecting his judgments to the appraisals of those most directly involved, he avoids the dangers inherent in decision-making in isolation.

All decisions finally made, the children to be changed are notified. How well this is handled determines the number of hours that need to be spent in explaining the move to the parents. If the child appreciates the fact that the change is made out of concern for his welfare, that the sending teacher is not rejecting him, that the receiving teacher is delighted to accept him, etc., then the prospect of serious and troublesome opposition is diminished. A pleasant chat with the principal, reassurances from the sending and receiving teachers—this kind of extra exertion makes for a smooth transition.

New Entrants

Our concern for proper placement must extend to those youngsters coming into our school from out-of-district schools. It is not in the spirit of things to place these incoming youngsters solely on the basis of class enrollment figures. Even if available, the records of new entrants should not satisfy our need to know certain specific abilities. Again, the use of the Informal Reading Inventory (or simply, the I.R.I.) is required. Routinely, the reading consultant administers this test of reading ability and makes recommendations for placement based on the test results. Since it would be unusual to have the reading consultant available at all times for this purpose, it is advantageous for the principal and his assistant (if he has one) to be able to give the inventory. In the event that circumstances prohibit the administering of the test prior to placement. then parents and child should be advised that the placement is tentative, subject to change.

The Informal Reading Inventory

Time and again the I.R.I. has been referred to as the best kind of reading tool for establishing individual instructional level. This information is essential to the proper functioning of an ungraded program. Since the I.R.I. is relatively simple in design and easy to administer, building administration should require each classroom teacher to learn its use.

There are I.R.I.s available commercially; however, a district may choose to develop its own. Ordinarily, selections are *not* taken from a reading series in use in the overall reading program. Short selections of from twenty-five to thirty words are excerpted from the pre-primers, about fifty words from the primers and first readers, increasing to approximately 150 words from the intermediate books. In order to provide material of about average difficulty for the level, the excerpts are best selected from the center part of the book.

Children are tested individually by having them read the excerpts, starting from the point about two levels below the expected level of competency.

The general procedure used is similar to the procedure for a reading activity in the textbook:

1. *Motivate.* Through discussion, stimulate the child's interest in the material to be read.
2. *Have child read silently.* As child reads, note reading behavior (squinting, frowning, finger-pointing, lip movements). These are clues of child's degree of comfort with the material.
3. *Have child read orally.* Count errors. Repeated errors (same word) are counted only once.
4. *Have child answer questions to check comprehension.*

Seventy-five percent is minimum for comprehension; ninety-five percent is minimum for pronunciation. When a child gets to the selection where he scores below those percentages, he is at frustration level. When he attains these minimum percentages, requiring help in only 4 or 5 words in a hundred, he is at his instructional level. When he scores close to 100% in both tests, he is at his independent level.

The Tri-Basal System of Reading

A distinguishing characteristic of the ungraded program is the opportunity provided pupils for growth in small steps. When reviewing material descriptive of any continuous progress plan in reading, the classic illustration, two-sided, depicts on one side children struggling to move from one grade level to the next (large, difficult steps); on the other side are children moving easily from one small level to the next (see Illustrations 1 and 2 on pp. 72 and 73.)

The tri-basal system of reading in operation at the Parkway School actually permits teachers to select steps of varying degrees, according to the teachers' understanding of their pupils' rates of progress. In certain situations, the classroom teacher may decide to move a group of children laterally, that is, to take them from a text at one level and, after completion, move them to a different

Illustrations by Phoebe Witte

72

PROGRESS IN THE UNGRADED ELEMENTARY SCHOOL BY LEVELS AND ACCORDING TO ABILITY

text at about the same level. Or, a teacher may move a group to the next higher level of the same series. A third alternative is to move a group to a level somewhat more difficult, yet not a full step. This flexibility comes from having several series or reading texts used according to a specific plan.

Although publishers of series of reading texts usually identify the levels of reading 2^1, 2^2, 3^1, 3^2, etc., scrutinization of vocabulary, sentence length, sentence structure, length of story, etc. will show consistent differences among the series in terms of difficulty. After a thorough study of various series of texts by the district reading director, three series were selected as "the basic three." One was a relatively easy series, hereafter referred to as the *fundamental* series; another was designated the *average;* the third was labelled the *advanced.*

Beginning in his first year of primary school, each child is assigned to a particular series depending upon his evident abilities at that time. Routinely, the pupil moves from one level to the next higher level within the assigned series, i.e., from fundamental 1^1 to fundamental 1^2 to fundamental 2^1, and so forth. If at any time his progress warrants only a lateral move, he may be given work at about the same level using a fourth series (called a supplementary basal).

A student may be moved to a higher level (but not quite a full step) by moving him from the fundamental to the average series, or from the average to the advanced at the same level designation. In all instances, teacher judgment is required, at times reinforced

---

Student

A . . . Fundamental 1^1 to Fund. 1^2 to Fund. 2^1 to Fund. 2^2 to Fund. 3^1
B . . . Fund. 1^1 to Avg. 1^1 to Fund. 1^2 to Fund. 2^1 to Avg. 2^1 to Avg. 2^2
C . . . Fund. 1^1 to Supplementary 1^1 to Avg. 1^1 to Fund. 1^2 to Fund. 2^1
D . . . Avg. 1^1 to Avg. 1^2 to Advanced 1^2 to Avg. 2^1 to Avg. 2^2 to Avg. 3^1
E . . . Adv. 1^1 to Adv. 1^2 to Adv. 2^1 to Adv. 2^2 to Adv. 3^1 to Adv. 2^2
F . . . Adv. 1^1 to Avg. 1^2 to Adv. 1^2 to Adv. 2^1 to Avg. 2^2 to Adv. 2^2
No attempt was made in the above to show *rate of progress.*

by the opinion of the reading consultant. The possibilities are limited only by the realities of the school situation. Listed below are some ways youngsters could advance through the program.

The classroom teacher faces certain questions repeatedly.

Should another reading group be formed?

Is additional refinement in grouping actually required?

Should a child (or two) be moved to another classroom?

Is it better to postpone refinement to escape the other alternatives?

Ultimately the needs of the students in question as well as the skills of the teacher will determine the decision.

The intent of the tri-basal system, as described, is to provide a maximum degree of flexibility in supplying pupils with the reading materials most suited to their real abilities. Additionally, it offers teachers a vast number of alternatives for adjusting their reading programs to the real progress of their students.

A Comprehensive and Balanced Reading Program

Perhaps in the narrower sense, a description of a comprehensive plan of reading is not related obviously to the notion of continuous progress. Yet, in this book, it is in keeping with the contention that the successful ungraded program is one that is viewed and implemented most broadly. Reading in the Parkway School is organized around the following five areas of instruction: (1) basic reading skills, (2) reading study skills, (3) oral reading, (4) literature, and (5) recreational reading. Further, it is recognized that the processes of learning to read take place not only during the formal reading period but are an integral part of all subject areas and school activities. The objectives of the reading program then are not confined to the *mechanics* of reading but are concerned with improvement of all activities involving reading, and with the total development of the individual·

Basic Reading Skills. In this area the foremost goal is to equip the individual with those skills which are common to all reading situations: (a) building of a basic vocabulary, (b) learning word attack skills, (c) understanding that which is read, and (d) reading with reasonable speed.

Reading Study Skills. To adequately handle the materials in the various curricular areas, these abilities should be developed: (a) getting the main idea, (b) taking notes, (c) outlining and summarizing, (d) retaining ideas read, (e) locating and using various types of reference materials, and (f) adjusting reading rate to the specific purpose.

Oral Reading. Instruction in oral reading is intended to: (a) develop a pleasant voice, (b) improve enunciation, (c) improve pronunciation, (d) develop poise and self-confidence in the oral situation, and (e) stimulate the listener.

Literature. To develop student appreciation of worthwhile literature is a major aim of this aspect of reading. Exposure to superior expressive styles should result in an increase in student sensitivity to and approval of the power of words and phrases. Beyond this, the content of the literary material should be able to fill, to some degree, the child's need for vicarious experiences. The child's range of interests may well be increased. Finally, certain of the literary materials serve as valuable aids in the building of social, moral, and ethical concepts.

Recreational Reading. In free reading, the student has the opportunity to investigate new fields, new ideas, to develop new tastes, all of which serve to demonstrate to the student the pleasures of reading. To accomplish this, the school is obliged to provide a wide variety of reading material, on all appropriate levels of difficulty; and the school must provide a portion of its time for this activity.

Many materials are needed to affect a reading program having such extensive aims. The basal texts, even in a multi-basal system, do not satisfy the ravenous appetite for materials inherent in such a program. The accompanying workbooks are standard equipment, also. Supplementary phonics workbooks are needed to enable a more intensive development of word attack skills and as material for individualized assignments. The reading laboratories on the market have proved excellent as supplementary material. These latter have been accepted widely as tools for a highly individualized program, successfully reinforcing the mechanical skills, increasing speed, and improving comprehension. Some of these laboratories are designed for intensive work on comprehension; others foster increased speed and improvement of study skills.

Yet, with all of these, a skimpy library and a poor library program would detrimentally affect the comprehensive program. To be sure, children learn by reading. They need to practice the skills that they acquire. They need to derive satisfaction, indeed pleasure, from the utilization of their skills. This promotes greater learning if we accept the definition of learning which says that learning takes place when the learner is performing an act which leads to a pleasant consequence.

The Parkway School has not been able to adopt any of the proferred learn-to-read-quick schemes that are proposed from time to time. The *single* solution is a temptation to which we cannot yield. for in each of them we have discovered flaws. Rather, we believe that some of our materials work well for some of our students, but not for all. Therefore, we have acquired a wide variety of reading implements, and we are investigating others. They are our tools, available as we need them. The program in one class with a particular age group is not the same in the adjoining classroom with a similar age group. The children are not the same, nor are their needs, nor is the teacher's judgment . . . and these must be reckoned with.

Only some slight reflection leads one to acknowledge that the materials, in full array, suffer debilitation at the hands of an incompetent teacher. The more demanding the program, the greater the need for the skilled professional. Those of us who have had to search for "the best" know full well the difficulties of the search. Nor can we look to the highly-touted self-teaching materials. They have not succeeded in replacing the teacher.

The Role of the Reading Specialist

The reading consultant should play a major part in overseeing the operation of the complex and more effective reading program. On the other hand, the value of this specialist may be (and too frequently is) dissipated by poor utilization of his talents.

Those districts that would proudly declare that they have the plain and ordinary *remedial* reading teachers of "the good old days" do themselves and their students a great disservice. Examine the contrasting responsibilities of the remedial reading teacher and the reading consultant.

If the specialist's time is spent exclusively or largely in working directly with youngsters who have been designated as remedial reading cases, then he will have an effect only on those specific students. In a school housing 1,000 students, this might amount to 50 to 100 students, or between five and ten percent of the total student body. What is happening to those same students when they are not with the specialist?

What else might the reading specialist do? He might observe the reading programs in each of the classrooms and follow up these visits with teacher-specialist conferences. At this time he could make suggestions on the various phases of the program, from selection and use of materials to the planning of independent activities. There might be demonstration teaching stemming from an observed teacher need. The role would not be that of supervisor, complete with authority, but rather as fellow teacher able to give special assistance.

New teachers, whether from other districts or simply of the beginning variety, need a longer period of orientation than can be supplied by building administration. The reading specialist, in the role of 'mother hen,' can take these several people and arrange a more comfortable and extensive break-in period, complete with observations, conferences, and demonstrations. Proper habits of instruction, as desired by the hiring district, would more probably be established.

The reading specialist does not work independently, of course. Under the direction of the building principal, he makes recommendations for budget items, helps plan the use of existing materials that need sharing (reading laboratories), advises the principal of the overall needs of the building as related to the reading program. As a supervisor, the principal is able also to ferret out special needs and can assign the specialist to care for them.

In the earliest part of the school year, the reading consultant's responsibilities are particularly burdensome—and essential to an effective reading program: orientation of new staff, working cooperatively with each teacher in establishing appropriate reading groups, selection and distribution of reading materials, early treatment of problems.

And what of remedial reading?

In a reading program based upon the concept of continuous progress, where grade labels do not exist, the likelihood of *sore thumbs* within the classroom is greatly lessened, if not entirely eliminated. Nevertheless, we inevitably have with us the youngsters whose progress in the various areas of reading is unsatisfactory, all factors considered. Special approaches may be needed. Who will give this extra measure of attention?

Classroom teachers refer these special cases to the reading consultant. A list is developed, a schedule evolves. On a regular basis the reading consultant goes to the classroom to work directly with the *remedial* youngsters during the regular period of reading. Initially, the classroom teacher is an observer. As work progresses, the classroom teacher participates. Eventually, the classroom teacher assumes full responsibility for instruction; however, the consultant keeps advised of progress and is always available for continued assistance.

This approach has the advantages of a program specifically planned for the remedial pupil by the reading specialist; additionally, it provides training for the classroom teacher who finally must accept responsibility for instruction. The reading specialist, when unfettered, resumes the many other practices in support of the total school reading program. All children profit. Classroom teachers become more proficient in reading instruction. The school administration gets maximum mileage from the board of education's investment.

A Greater Need for Planning

When the classroom teacher is required to plan an instructional program based upon the specific abilities of the youngsters within class, it is indeed vastly different from placing the youngsters within a program that is already in existence (the first grade program, the second grade program, etc.). In the latter instance, teachers have been known to use the same plan book, modifying it slightly and reluctantly, somehow enduring the frustrations of having to shoehorn the "misfits" into the ill-fitting slots. (How many Cinderellas can there be?)

The ungraded program makes it necessary for former second grade teachers to use tools that heretofore had been used exclusively by first grade teachers, or third grade teachers. The number of teacher editions of the various text and workbooks needed is usually doubled. All classroom teachers find this true. While it is difficult to give an answer to the question of extra expenses entailed through ungrading, in this situation it is very definite. To plan effectively, teachers must have a substantially greater number of teacher guides, at each of the levels likely to be encountered in their teaching.

A teacher usually identifies his reading groups and maps out a weekly plan for each of them. The plans reflect a concern for the five reading areas previously noted. An important part of the planning is the development of independent activities. If these are selected haphazardly, there will be wasted time and probable interference with the teacher as he works directly with one of the groups. The activities must include work that can be accomplished without the direct assistance of the teacher, without simply being busywork, and it must relate to the specific needs of the children. It is not necessary that the independent activities be always related to reading.

Groups within the classroom do not remain static. There may be movement up or down, as ability dictates. Groups within groups may be formed. Several students within a group may need additional skill work that others do not. These might be assigned particular selections from a phonics workbook. Depending on the difficulty of the assignment, children may work independently or under the direct guidance of the teacher. In other situations, members from each of the groups may work together in uncovering information about a topic in which all have a special interest. This would probably be a library assignment. In this case classroom teacher and librarian would plan their parts cooperatively. Other situations might allow one student versed in a particular technique to assist others who need special tutoring. Undoubtedly, there would be many occasions for individual assignments.

The various laboratories referred to previously are excellent tools for individual work, especially at the higher levels of the elementary school. Experience shows, however, that independent assignments lose much of their effectiveness when the teacher fails to periodically and carefully evaluate the quality of the student effort.

WITHIN THE INTER-AGE CLASSES

This aspect of the ungraded plan seems to provoke the greatest amount of interest. If there is a mixture of second and third year primary students, does this require the teacher to teach both second and third grade? Or first and second grade when the combination is such?

Applied to the reading segment of the class program, the question is resolved most obviously. There are no grades. Therefore, the abilities of the children are determined, the groups are set, and instruction within the classroom is planned accordingly. Variations occur as a result of the children's rates of progress.

Are social studies, science, and mathematics treated similarly? What about other portions of language arts?

The ungraded school is not a specific technique but rather a philosophy subject to interpretation. Thus, we find a variety of practices in effect in the ungraded schools throughout the country. Three general ways of coping with instruction in the ungraded school (other than reading) are examined in the next few paragraphs. Since experience frequently dictates a change in procedure, it would serve little purpose to identify the specific districts utilizing each procedure. Simply, these methods are in use, or have been used.

Afternoon Re-Grouping

This procedure is used with the inter-age classes *and* with all ungraded classes. Mornings are utilized for instruction in reading and other phases of language arts within the assigned homeroom. In the afternoons, children are dispersed for instruction in the other subject areas. Group placement for mathematics depends primarily on ability. In science and social studies the newer groupings depend upon previous exposure (years in school) and this, of course, permits age grouping again.

The teachers of the afternoon subjects are not specialists. They are the instructors of the morning who have split up the afternoon assignments.

Re-Grouping Within the Self-Contained Classroom—A

The math program within the inter-age class calls for ability grouping, the number of groups determined by the range within the class and the ability of the teacher to manage such groups. If previous exposure does bring these groups closer to being same-age groups, it is a matter of circumstance, not design. A suitable range of instructional materials is required and in generous quantities.

When the courses of study for science and social studies are founded on the year-level idea, closely or entirely following a textbook series, the instruction in these areas is separated along these lines, catering to the children's previous exposure.

Re-Grouping Within the Self-Contained Classroom—B

Here again, the math program calls for ability grouping, age not a factor. However, in the areas of social studies and science, revised curricula permits crossing age lines. Progress is measured by ability to handle materials of graduated degrees of complexity. All pupils might work on the same general unit, but their group or individual assignments are suited to their levels of sophistication. Beyond the full class treatment of the studied topic, there would evolve grouping for interest, by ability, team learning groups, tutorial grouping (student helping student), and individual assignment.

In team learning groups, students are set up in learning teams, in the manner of the Durrell pupil team learning plan. Two, three, or more students, ready to work together on a given unit, are given the materials on that unit. After a period of working together, when the students judge that they have mastered the unit, they present themselves to the teacher for testing.

In tutorial grouping, one child, having mastery of a particular unit, works closely with one or more pupils having need of additional help. The tutoring pupil is given specific instructions by the teacher, including materials and procedures to use.

A Flexible Elementary Science Program

A curriculum guide may be used which provides for pupils of different abilities to work on the same topic but at levels suited to those abilities. To illustrate, the science guide used throughout the Plainview-Old Bethpage school district is described.

On the elementary level, science is divided into five major categories, as follows: (1) Plants, (2) Animals, (3) The Human Body, (4) The Earth, and (5) Matter and Energy. Other categories of science such as astronomy, meteorology, and microbiology are treated as sub-categories.

Each year children are exposed to each of the major categories. However, the specific assignments given are based on individual pupil ability. This is made possible by identifying seven levels of complexity, under each of the major units. Additionally, there are many suggested enrichment activities for each of the levels. Thus, while one group of children within a class may be doing work on Plants, level 2, another group may be doing work on the same unit. but at level 4. It is the teacher's role to select the level of complexity required in order to adapt the class work to the real abilities of the individual students.

The teacher's development of each unit is guided also by three professional books which are referred to frequently in the district guide and which are supplied to each elementary teacher.[2]

In this approach there is no single text for a class. Various texts are used and at appropriate levels of difficulty.

While the district science guide is especially helpful in making inter-age grouping workable, it is, in fact, in use in all classes as an instrument for individualization.

The following material has been extracted from the science guide. It illustrates one of the major categories, MATTER AND ENERGY, for use with Levels Kindergarten, One and Two; then, within the same category, it shows study and activities for Levels Two, Three, and Four. While the references, as listed, cannot be

---

[2] Blough, Schwartz, and Huggett. *Elementary School Science and How to Teach It.* New York: Holt, Rinehart, and Winston, Inc., 1958; Craig, Gerald S. *Science for the Elementary School Teacher.* New York: Ginn and Company, 1958; Navarra and Zaffaroni. *Science Today for the Elementary School Teacher.* Illinois: Row, Peterson, and Company, 1960.

interpreted by the reader without the bibliography found in the
guide, it has been left in to demonstrate how the classroom teacher
is encouraged to use a wide variety of sources.

Selected Excerpts from the Central District No. 4 Science Guide

Matter and Energy: Levels Kindergarten, One, and Two
A. What are some materials?
  1. Why is stone sometimes used in building foundations?
    a. Why will it hold up heavy loads?
    b. Will stone float?
  2. Does man make stone?
    a. What are cement blocks?
    b. What are bricks?
    c. What is concrete?
  3. Why are many parts of a house made of wood?
    a. Is wood easy to cut?
    b. Is wood easy to nail?
    c. Is wood easy to bend and to smooth?
  4. How is wood different from stone?
    a. Was it ever alive?
    b. Will wood rot? rust? burn?
    c. Will wood float?
  5. What are the physical properties of other materials used
     in houses, such as glass, copper, aluminum, and steel?

B. What is a chemical change?
  1. What happens when oxygen combines with iron?
  2. What happens when wood combines with oxygen?
  3. Can we put the changed materials back into their original
     forms?

C. In what ways is heat important to us?
  1. How does temperature affect our lives?
  2. How can we observe differences in temperature?
  3. How can we measure differences in temperature?
  4. What happens to water when it becomes very cold?
  5. What happens to water when it becomes very hot?

D. What is a magnet?
  1. What materials does a magnet attract?
  2. How can we make our own magnet?
  3. How is a temporary magnet different from a permanent
     magnet?

    4. How can magnets make our work easier?
    5. How do magnets help ships at sea?

E. How is electricity used in your home?
    1. What does it light?
    2. What does it heat?
    3. What does it cool?
    4. How many machines does it run?
    5. How is it carried into your home?
    6. Can it do harm?
       a. Can it cause fire?
       b. Why is it unsafe to play with electric wires, appliances, and outlets?

F. What can we learn about machines?
    1. What is work?
       a. What kind of work do you do?
       b. How can we make work easier?
    2. How are things moved?
       a. Is it easier to slide or roll things?
       b. How does a wheel make work easier?
       c. How does a ramp make work easier?
    3. How are things lifted?
    4. How are things lifted and moved?
    5. What are the machines that work for us in our home?

REFERENCES

For items A and B.. 1. Reference no. 33, pp. 43-80
                         2.   10, pp. 371-381
                         3.   17, pp. 281-284

For item C.............. 1. Reference no. 33, pp. 113-122
                         2.   10, pp. 397-402, 412-418
                         3.   17, pp. 666-672

For items D and E..... 1. Reference no. 33, pp. 128-130, 149-163
                         2.   10, pp. 467-473, 480-488
                         3.   17, pp. 716-730, 755-764, 7

For item F................ 1. Reference no. 35, pp. 30-31 (Manual T/Ed
                         2.   33, pp. 15-28
                         3.   10, pp. 444-451, 455-461
                         4.   17, pp. 658-665, 681-691

Matter and Energy: Levels Two, Three, and Four

A. What properties of matter can be observed?
  1. What can we observe about iron?
      a. Is iron strong?
      b. Can iron be bent into different shapes?
      c. Does iron rust, rot, or burn?
      d. Why are some parts of a house made of iron?
      Horizontal Exploration *
  * e. Why is iron combined with other metals?
  * f. What are the advantages of steel over iron?
  * g. What are the advantages of aluminum over iron?
  2. What can you observe about liquids?
      a. Can they become solids?
      b. Can they become gases?
  3. Can solids change?
  4. How does matter change when it is burned?
  5. How do things change when they rust?
  6. What other property changes can you observe?

B. How can magnets make work easier?
  1. What are lines of force?
  2. How many poles does a magnet have?
  3. Which part exerts the strongest pull?
  4. What kinds of things does a magnet attract?
      Horizontal Exploration *
  * 5. How are magnets used in our daily lives?
  * 6. What does the North Pole on earth mean? The South
      Pole?

C. What are the uses of electricity?
  1. What things work by electricity?
  2. How does electricity make light?
  3. How does electricity make heat?
  4. How does electricity move things?
      Horizontal Exploration *
  * 5. How can we make an electromagnet?
  * 6. What is a circuit? a short circuit?
  * 7. How can we stop a flow of electricity?

D. How do machines make work easier?
  1. What are some simple machines?
      a. Wheel
      b. Lever

   c. Inclined plane

     Horizontal Exploration *

 *d. Wheel and axle

 *e. Gear

 * f. Pulley

 *g. Wedge

 *h. Screw

2. What is movement?
3. What causes friction?
4. Why is it easier to move things on a smooth surface than on a rough one?
5. When and how is friction desirable?
6. What are some ways of reducing friction?
   a. What effect do rollers have on friction?
   b. What effect do wheels on axles have on friction?
   c. Why are wheels on axles better than rollers for moving things?
   d. What effect does oiling surfaces have on friction?
   e. What effect do ball bearings have on friction?
7. How do things move in water?
   a. How does pushing backward against the water affect motion?
   b. How does a fish swim through water? a squid? a person?
   c. How does the moving of arms, legs, or tails affect movement through water?
   d. How do boats move through water?
8. How do things move in air?
   a. How does pushing backward against air affect motion? downward?
   b. Does air exert pressure? In what directions?
   c. Can we use air pressure to move through air?
   d. How does a bird move through air?
   e. How do the different kinds of airplanes move through the air?
9. What kind of power was first used to do work?
10. How do we use wind power to make work easier?
11. How do we use water power to make work easier?

     Horizontal Exploration *

* 12. How does water power make electric power?
* 13. How is steam used for power?
* 14. How does a gasoline engine give us power?
* 15. How does a diesel engine give us power?

E. How do we hear sounds?
   1. How are sounds made?
   2. How are sounds different?
   3. How are sounds carried?
      Horizontal Exploration *
 * 4. How do the vibrations inside our ears cause us to hear?
 * 5. How do we determine the direction of sound?
 * 6. How can we prove that sound travels more slowly than light?

REFERENCES

(The format for references for each of the major items is the same as the previously-listed references.)

A Flexible Social Studies Program

As with the reading and the science programs, the social studies program employs a multi-text approach, utilizing a district development guide for suggested sequence of content. Again, from level to level there is overlapping of content. For example, Food, as a subject of study, is suggested by the guide for levels two and three. This being true, it can happen that the youngsters in an interage class can work on the same general topic. The teacher, in making assignments, differentiates those assignments on the basis of the previous exposure of the youngsters to the topic *and* on the real level of sophistication of the students.

It must be obvious that the kind of program called for is one that is especially dynamic, one that cannot readily be tied to a single series of textbooks. Teacher *must* have an awareness of pupil ability and sophistication as never before. There is a greater need for a wide assortment of materials, and these must always be added to, improved upon. Progress reports on each pupil must go beyond an indication that the child has been in school X number of years.

The major aim of any social studies program must not be a simple exposure to facts, dates, and figures, but rather the development of students' critical thinking, their skills of observation, methods of inquiry, and intelligent response to social happenings, local and world-wide. As this becomes the real focus, content takes on a lesser role, important, but only as the means for developing the social study skills.

Multi-level Spelling Programs

The twenty-words-a-week-for-all-members-of-the-class spelling program is outrageously improper within the school that purports to take individual differences into consideration. The effective program is individualized, allowing children to work at the level of difficulty suited to their abilities, and to progress according to their natural speed.

Newer materials are on the market which are designed to allow varying degrees of individualization. Most successful are those which simply contain lists graduated in terms of difficulty. Thus, there are several lists at level A, several more at level B, a greater number of lists at level C, etc. Parkway School uses *The Multi-Level Speller* by Morton Botel, published by Penns Valley Publishers, Inc., Pennsylvania.[3]

A placement test enables the teacher to designate the starting level for each of her children. At that level children are given weekly pre-tests that determine the words in the lists that need studying. If the child makes a large number of errors in the pre-test, then he might study only one list for that week; if he makes only one or two in a list then he may decide to study another and still another list. At the end of the week, he is tested. Those words not mastered are added to the following week's work.

Since there are likely to be many groups within each classroom, it is to the teacher's advantage to develop a system of operation wherein children learn to administer the tests to each other, in

[3] Note: The writer, in identifying the speller in use at Parkway School, does not wish to suggest that the speller is or is not the best available. Rather, it is the one in use that has proved successful. Its particular merit is its multi-level approach.

groups, in "buddy" fashion, or in various combinations. The teacher frequently checks on progress, usually sees to the mastery tests herself. It is a workable program. After a period of operation, its ability to promote success makes the inflexible program unacceptable.

THE SOCIAL ASPECTS OF THE INTER-AGE CLASS

In the early part of this chapter it was noted that there were some misgivings by the youngsters because of the inter-age mixings. Among the concerns, expressed or not, were:

"Did I get left back?"

"Are these bigger children going to bully me?"

"Are these younger children going to make me look silly?"

"Will my friends in the other classes make fun of me?"

Some tentative conclusions follow, resulting from experience:

1. Age "barriers" disappear with time. The opportunities for social exchange available in a "mixed" room helps eliminate those barriers.
2. Children seem to gravitate toward those of like ability and/or of similar temperament and interests, not necessarily those of similar age.
3. The inter-age groupings produce opportunities for leadership not otherwise available to certain children.
4. The tendency for older children to dominate the class situation may be controlled.
5. Generally, younger children are affected in a positive manner, academically and socially, by the age mixing.
6. The role played by the classroom teacher ultimately decides the effects of the inter-age mixing.

DESCRIPTION: ONE CLASS DURING ONE SCHOOL DAY

Visitors like to "see" the ungraded classroom. Those who expect *fireworks* or spectacle are disappointed. Those who anticipate teacher sensitivity to individual needs are more likely to find what they seek . . . provided there is a quality teacher in charge. Following is a brief description of a day's activities in an ungraded class.

8:45 - 9:00 Morning exercises, including flag salute, song, silent meditation, attendance, lunch count, and such.

9:00 - 9:20 Discussion of current events. Four children, previously assigned, give their reports. Others participate on voluntary basis. There is full class participation in discussion under teacher direction.

9:20 - 9:30 Before the start of class teacher had placed written directions on board regarding independent activities. For example:

Group I: Complete worksheets, 1 and 2 (these are teacher-made dittoes, exercises reinforcing phonics skills). Mary, George, Edward, Susan: Do pp. 18-19 of arithmetic workbook. Put completed work on my desk. (This is not new work, but exercises for needed reinforcement.)

All others: after completion of worksheets, select material from class library for free reading (recreational reading—books suited to class are on loan from school library).

Extra: Work on science project. (All children have been assigned science projects which require manipulation of materials, e.g., tin-can phones, water wheels, electro-magnets, and such.)

(Groups II and III are given similar assignments. In some instances, certain children will have work especially selected for them—perhaps make-up work in math or science. In other instances, children may be paired for drill work on addition facts, or multiplication facts using drill cards. In all cases the work selected is of a nature which enables the children to work independently, not requiring more than brief explanation.)

Prior to taking one group for reading instruction, the teacher orally explains the written directions, answers related questions, and makes reference to activities to be pursued in event of early completion of assignment.

9:30 - 9:55 Teacher works directly with first reading group. Usual procedure: motivation, silent reading, oral reading, discussion. Others doing silent independent activities.

9:55 - 10:00 Teacher directions, as needed, followed by setting up of next reading group.

10:00 - 10:25 Second group works directly with teacher, as above, except at different, more appropriate reading level. Others: independent activities, as described.

10:25 - 10:30 Teacher directions, as needed; organizing for Group III.

10:30 - 10:55 Teacher works with Group III. Others: independent activities.

10:55 - 11:00 Teacher collects written assignments. Class puts materials away, prepares for special activity.

11:00 - 11:40 Special activity (art, music, physical education, or library) under the direction of the specialist, but frequently with the active assistance and cooperation of the classroom teacher.

11:40 - 12:15 Creative writing activity (whole class) . . . Under teacher direction, children participate in discussion of possible stories that are suggested by an untitled magazine picture . . . and another. After sufficient motivation, children are assigned the development of a story from another untitled picture. Teacher gives individual help as needed, in the spelling of a word, in discussing an individual child's idea, in phrasing. Papers are collected (Errors in grammatical usage, spelling, etc. to be corrected by teacher at a later time; teacher will identify categories of errors for later group work. There will also be a follow-up lesson on the content of the pupil-made stories for overall appreciation of the children's own creative work.)

12:15 - 1:15 Lunch and recreation

1:15 - 1:55 Re-grouping within the class for math instruction. As with reading there is more than one math group. Again, teacher has made provision for independent activities. These will include drill work, workbook assignments, pupil helping pupil, perhaps the use of programmed materials, if available. (With two groups it is probable that the teacher will get the opportunity to work directly with both groups during the period; with more than two groups this might prove less likely. The effectiveness of the math program will hinge largely upon the quality of the independent assignments.)

1:55 - 2:05 Homework assignments given. These, too, should not be identical but must be differentiated, based on observed pupil needs.

2:05 - 2:40 Science: Continuation of unit on Animals. There are two major groups (ability), and under each there are sub-groups (interest). Leaders of the sub-groups give brief reports on progress in their special areas.

2:45 Dismissal.

The amount of time devoted to reading is not the same each day and probably should not be the same. At certain times, when the teacher has a need to spend additional time on other segments of the language arts, he might work directly with only two reading groups, or only one. The math period could be shortened or elongated, according to teacher judgment and class need. Science might be by-passed one or two days weekly in favor of social studies, or both subjects might be handled each day. It is, of course, the teacher's responsibility to give proper amounts of exposure to each subject area. The principal, in his supervision, in his collection and examination of plan books, must be sensitive to this.

In the description above, various kinds of ability groupings were illustrated, as were examples of opportunities for whole class instruction. individual assignments, and the like. This is the way of life in a classroom where the teacher is responsible for catering to individual abilities and needs. This is true in the rooms with inter-age groupings; this is equally true in the class which is not inter-age.

SUMMARY

The ungraded classroom features a program of reading based on the concept of continuous progress. For effective operation of the program, each child's instructional level must be accurately determined. Correction of errors in placement is best done at the beginning of the year. Other changes are made as required.

The Informal Reading Inventory is used for correctly establishing instructional level individually. New entrants should be given this placement test before assignment to a classroom.

A multi-basal system of reading provides maximum flexibility in moving children from one level to another. The most effective program of reading interprets reading in its broadest sense.

The reading consultant's role is a key one. His contributions are greatest when his duties are concerned with the overall reading program. Remedial instruction is provided for youngsters with special needs; however, the consultant develops individual programs, demonstrates special techniques, and eventually leaves the classroom teacher to carry out the program.

Properly implemented, the ungraded program reduces pressures on classroom teachers and pupils. It demands greater planning, more materials, and fuller attention to the changing needs of pupils.

Although the inter-age class attracts the most interest, the actual program is not dramatically different from that of any ungraded class.

In programs of math, science, and social studies, the ungraded school may utilize a modified form of departmentalization. Or, these programs may function within the self-contained classroom through varied classroom organizational techniques.

In general, the ungraded school demands flexibility: constant grouping and re-grouping within the class, changes in pupil classroom placement as needed, and refinement of individual programs as progress is made.

4

The Team Approach

An important attribute of the ungraded school is the flexibility it permits. So contend the proponents, and rightfully so. For instance, the ungraded school, as described to this point, permits placement of any child within the larger ungraded unit, as opposed to the smaller grade units. Further, teachers may teach, and are expected to teach, according to the abilities of children as opposed to the narrower concept of teaching a grade program. In both instances opportunity is provided to adapt to the realities of whatever situations present themselves. The hampering restrictions are removed.

Yet, if flexibility is desirable, can the inquiring educator be content knowing there are other methods of attaining this objective? What *kinds* of flexibility are reasonably possible, or needed?

In broadest terms, flexibility must be sought that enables the surmounting of all instructional problems, that enables, even promotes, quality of instruction.

The innovation known as *team teaching* deals creatively with three basic units of instruction, specifically: People, Space, and Time. These units are dealt with in such a way as to render them elastic, responsive to different instructional needs. At first, the expressed intention of the plan was to remedy or alleviate some of the secondary school's problems related to over-crowding. In practice, it was found that sound implementation of some of the inherent ideas was able to improve time-worn instructional practices. Frequently, however, the earlier aim, to effect economies, is rejected entirely; the sole purpose of using any part of the program is to improve instruction.

Before exploring any formal team teaching plan, each of the basic instructional units are considered separately. How have they been ordinarily employed? What modifications may be made in their utilization?

When a school leaps from a formal plan to a radical departure, it may attract the confusion, resistance, and poor performance that often accompany rapid change. There are gradual steps leading easily to a full-fledged team teaching instructional pattern. These are considered initially in this chapter. The more formalized approach is then regarded. Finally, we note the easy blending of team teaching and the ungraded school.

AN INFORMAL LOOK: PEOPLE, SPACE, AND TIME

Within the Sacred Portals

In the ordinary elementary classroom, it is usual for the classroom teacher to close the door behind the last entering pupil. Thereafter, the classroom becomes an island, a unit unto itself, invasions thereto rare and of short duration. Whatever happens within the walls of that classroom, good, bad, and mediocre, has an impact limited, generally, to the room's occupants.

The insecure teacher derives the greatest satisfaction from this arrangement. Those few instances, during the year, of formal observation by the principal, do produce a temporary state of palpitation and panic; but, the infrequency of the occasion makes this form of indignation bearable.

Contradictory as it may seem, limited exposure to observation is most apt to indulge the apprehensions of the wary teacher. If the teacher's role were to require a stream of visitors, and this were known, acceptance would become a matter of course. Fears would dissipate in most instances. Teaching performance would be likely to improve. It is difficult to justify an indiscriminately-selected *stream of visitors* as a means of stimulating the teacher's exhibition of finest skill. There are sound reasons, however, for increasing exposure to fellow professionals.

The building principal who witnesses the teaching of arithmetic lessons in half a dozen classes is bound to prefer one teaching style over another. He may discover one teacher of the group who is a master of working with small groups. Another teacher may be able to creatively employ some rather prosaic materials to great advantage. A third member of the group may have particular success in developing pupil motivation.

How does the supervisor bring about the sharing of these strengths, to the fullest advantage of the entire school? It may be that he provokes discussion on the topic of arithmetic at a faculty meeting and then takes the opportunity to highlight some of the good teaching he has seen (diplomatically, we hope). Yet, what have the many burdens of administration prevented him from seeing that was as good or better? Would it not be more effective for teachers to *see* the good teaching?

The demonstration lesson at the end of a school day, using selected children, has disadvantages. It is difficult, perhaps impossible, to recapture the spirit of an ongoing class situation. The unnatural quality of the lesson produces strain on the teacher, the children involved, and on the imaginations of the observers.

Similarly, what is the reaction of a faculty witnessing a model lesson via 16mm film? The questions are inevitably asked:

"How many takes did this require?"

"Would you say that the children were hand-picked?"

The cynicism stems from the suspicion that model lessons work best under model conditions, that under real conditions a lesson would progress quite differently.

Paying heed to faculty preference for reality, the building principal who wants his staff exposed to good teaching must search out the possible and the practical means of achieving that objective. In some few instances, teachers may be sent to schools outside their own district to view actual, possibly exotic, instructional programs. There is value in this, to be sure, as there is value in seeing after-school demonstration lessons or in viewing movies, or Educational TV tapes, of model teaching. The viewing teacher, nevertheless, too often feels the disappointment of having seen a lesson or program not closely enough related to his own.

The outside visit is also an expensive procedure, requiring a substitute and travel costs. Moreover, the teacher's absence negatively affects his own instructional program, for substitutes may not be expected to carry on an instructional plan with the continuity and effectiveness of the regular teacher.

By process of elimination, the solution becomes increasingly obvious. Teachers ought to be able to see good teaching within the confines of the building they serve, within the hours that are designated as the teaching day. (It must be assumed that good teaching does take place.) The sacred portals must open wide in welcome, to permit sharing to promote unity.

How may this be arranged? Which teachers will observe? Who will be the observed? When will the observations take place? Who is caring for the observing teacher's class? Is there need for formal follow-up procedures? There are other questions.

THE PRINCIPAL'S ROLE

Determining Need

The building principal who takes time to visit the classroom, to observe programs in action, and who seeks to bring about improvement in instruction through this very basic technique, is in a position to determine the individual weaknesses and strengths of each of his staff. The teacher who feels somewhat ineffectual in the actual exercising of the multi-level spelling program would certainly find profit in viewing the procedures employed by the teacher who is smoothly and comfortably running the program. The teacher who has never actually made use of the overhead projector might be happily made aware of the potentialities of the machine. The teacher particularly competent in science might welcome the opportunity to exhibit his special skills.

Step one in a program to promote intra-visitation, then, would be for the principal to determine which teachers would profit from exposure to other teachers' instructional methods, and to select the specific areas where weaknesses were most apparent. After the determinations are made, the wheels may be set in motion.

The Soft Sell

The principal who bullishly arranges for the "poor" teacher to watch the "better" teacher is going to suffer the obvious results of intimidation. Instead, the principal must approach the entire staff in the manner of the administrator with a mission: the sharing and distribution of the professional wealth, for the profit of all. The points to make: (1) we all have special professional attributes that the principal is able to witness from time to time which would be of benefit to those who possess valuable but different talents; (2) the sharing of our skills with each other would benefit us all professionally and would ultimately benefit all the children, which is the reason for our service in the district; (3) sharing, in the fashion mentioned, would promote a unity of system.

It is difficult for teachers to feel a gross resistance to an idea which is intended as a means of improving the school program, and where teachers are not offended by authoritarian tactics. Teachers should definitely participate, to the extent possible, in the selection of classes to visit, programs to be observed. Teachers to be visited should be made aware that their special skills have made them valuable resource people. At one time or another every teacher should be an observer and an observed teacher.

Arranging the Visit

There is no procedure that can apply to all schools; however, a number of suggestions are made, some of which can be utilized. The special teacher (the librarian, the vocal music teacher, the art teacher and such) may have their schedules altered—infrequently—in order that they might cover the visiting teacher's class for the period of the visit. Or, during the time when the special teacher has control of his class, the regular classroom teacher may take the opportunity to visit. If the idea can be sold to the superintendent and the board, then a substitute can be hired from time to time, for the sole purpose of relieving a half-dozen or more teachers during the course of the day to allow visitation. The principal and/or his assistant may take on the role of the substitute in some instances.

Whatever means are employed, the teacher to be visited and the visiting teacher should have mutually agreed upon the time, the length of stay, the purposes, and the follow-through. In the earliest of these meetings, the principal should be directly involved, helping to define each of the points listed, demonstrating his own real interest in the idea. As the project progresses, it is of greater value to have the teachers make the arrangements themselves, requesting the assistance of the building administration only as needed. The demonstration of initiative is an indication of the teachers' acceptance.

The Follow-Through

Greater advantage is likely when there is an opportunity for some kind of follow through. At the full faculty meeting the experiences of staff should be discussed. The principal asks: "How have you profited?" "Have the arrangements been unsatisfactory?" "Can you make suggestions for improvement?"

There should be opportunity for observer and observed to discuss the observed lesson privately, to go over such items as: What preceded the lesson? Is Henry a slow-learner? May I see the outcome of the lesson? Does homework help?

The Principal's Persistence

It is not easy to break the tradition of the sacred portal. Unless the principal persists for a period of time, several weeks, or even months, teachers will tend to revert to the security of the closed door. To avoid this, he must keep his hand in the planning, the arranging, and the overall progress of the idea.

Expanding a Good Idea

One teacher learns to respect another's prowess in the teaching of science. Is he likely to say, "How about introducing this to my class for me?" It may be a lesson in astronomy, or biology, where the expert has had special training. If several classes are to receive exposure to this topic, and if space is available for a large group, would it be feasible for the expert to give the introductory lesson for the entire group?

Previous to the large group lesson, as a means of making it most effective, the teachers not directly involved with the introduction might prepare certain materials for the lesson. These would be specified by the instructor of the large group. Additionally, he would advise them of his plans, perhaps making suggestions for follow-up.

Since there is no one rigid interpretation of *team teaching*, there is no reason why the above effort could not be cited as an example of one aspect of the idea. One teacher served as the master teacher; several teachers were involved in the planning. There was a large group lesson which was followed by instruction in smaller class-size units.

A science lesson was used as an example; however, any subject area might lend itself to this treatment, according to the real needs of the school.

The Matter of Time

It is not usual for the elementary school to rigidly delineate time allotments for each of the subject areas. Such delineation would conflict with the principle of adjustment to individual differences. Nevertheless, those teachers who impose upon themselves a sharply-defined schedule would find a need for elasticity as they began to participate in joint ventures in instruction.

In the case of the elementary school that employed a departmentalized program, it would be necessary to make adjustments to allow longer or shorter periods of time as dictated by need.

Faults in the traditional closed door policy of the classroom are apparent. Teacher strengths ought to be shared. Better and more efficient instruction is possible when teachers plan together, when school spaces and time are used more creatively.

For emphasis, the following points are repeated: Teachers are apt to support a program when they are given the opportunity to give it full consideration, when they play a part in ideation; conversely, they will balk, as is the wont of proud people, when projects, good or bad, are forced upon them. For that reason the period of exploration is highly desirable. The interim steps serve to establish a sound base for the more formal program.

MORE FORMALLY: A TEAM PLAN

A Pattern for Effective Instruction

Before delving into the specifics of the formal team plan, we should examine the purposes of exploring this change of instructional pattern. There is growing pressure for increased academic achievement on all levels. At the elementary level, the self-contained classroom—where one teacher teaches nearly all subjects to his assigned group of children within his assigned classroom—has again had its inherent weaknesses subjected to criticism. Specifically, it is doubted that one teacher can teach all subjects to all children with equal effectiveness and skill. A teacher might be strong in the language arts area but weak in science, or math. Yet, on that same level of instruction there might be a neighboring teacher with special skill in science and/or math. It is argued that, under the pattern of the self-contained classroom, groups of children are, in effect, penalized in particular subject areas by the circumstances of not being exposed to the skills of the teachers most knowledgable in those subject areas.

Other questions are posed about the size of pupil groups. How large a group can a teacher handle effectively? Should not the lesson itself, or the subject taught, or the ability of the teacher determine size?

Through departmentalization, schools have been able to capitalize more on the subject-matter strengths of teachers, but they have lost out on flexibility, at least.

In effect, a team approach appears as a compromise plan. This is more true when the team is not employed at all times as a team, but only from time to time as needs dictate, or perhaps, as circumstances allow.

The Make-Up of a Team

For purposes of illustration, let us examine one possible team organizational plan: a five-classroom unit where the teachers have mutually agreed to work and plan together for the instruction of 140 children of the intermediate level. Ordinarily, these are teachers of self-contained classes, each having 28 youngsters.

Assisting the team from time to time, according to need, are the school librarian, a school clerk, and a substitute teacher. Help might be secured from any member of the teaching staff at special times. The psychologist, the art teacher, a member of administration might fill a special role. Thus, the personnel resource for the team is the total faculty.

One member of the "regular" team would be designated *the team leader*. The effectiveness of this leader would determine, largely, the effectiveness of the team. This person might be appointed by the principal, or he might be selected by the group. Some schools choose to develop a system of rotation so that all members of the team experience the leader role.

The duties and responsibilities of a team leader include:

1. Chairing of team meetings, including the development of the agenda, and the preparation of minutes.
2. Communicating with the members of the regular team, the occasionally invited members, and the building administration in order to carry out the group plans.
3. Coordination of all activities required for the execution of an instructional unit.

The above duties are general, encompassing broad responsibilities. These may be delegated to other members of the team by the leader on occasion, but the overall responsibility remains with the leader. Of necessity, the team leader assumes a role of authority, and is constantly required to render decisions for the team; these might best be made in democratic fashion, but the decisions will come through him.

A Team Project

As an example of a team project, let us assume that the team has selected a specific unit for team action. The first act of the team would be the planning of the unit. In the planning, the team would determine the content, the objectives of the unit, a tentative time schedule, the kinds of materials to be used, the personnel needed —including resource people outside the regular team—the kinds of groupings to be employed. This phase of the work would undoubtedly take a number of meetings, even before the first act of instruction. To assist the team, a clerk would be utilized for taking notes and for handling all details of a clerical nature.

Throughout the planning period, the teachers would gear their plans to specific pupil needs. Questions would be raised, the answers then determining the particulars of the plans:

To what parts of the content should all pupils be exposed?

Which pupils are able to work independently effectively?

What are the reading materials best suited to the slower-learning children?

What relevant audio-visual materials are available?

Which pupils need special help in developing the various study skills, i.e., note-taking, outlining, extracting information, etc.?

What resource people could be called upon for their special talents?

On the basis of the teachers' knowledge of pupils' individual abilities and needs, the team could determine those aspects of the lesson to which all pupils could profitably be exposed (the large group lessons for all pupils of the five-classroom unit), where small or individual lessons would be required, where independent activity was desirable, etc. In all the cited instances, the team could then determine the size of the instructional units and the kinds of individualization of instruction. There would be grouping, re-grouping, and further re-grouping, accordingly. The desired kind of interaction between teachers, pupils, and materials would determine the specific instructional techniques, e.g.:

Lecture	Discussion, small group
Debate	Committee work
Oral recitation	Oral drill
Panel discussion	Workbook activity
Use of films, radio, tape	Library research
Independent reading	Written tests

Prior to the initiation of the unit, the team would determine the desirability of formal testing before and after the unit as a means

of measuring the effectiveness of the completed unit. In most instances, a less formal procedure is found satisfactory. The teacher-
made test might be administered to all pupils at the completion of
the unit. While measuring individual pupil progress, it would also
give indication of the effectiveness of the team effort.

One of the foremost characteristics of the team teaching program
is the large degree of interaction among participating team members. Thus it is often true that each lesson is subjected to intensive
analysis by members of the team. They constantly review what they
have done, discuss the shortcomings and the virtues of each step
taken, and probably make more corrections in succeeding efforts
than would have been true under the closed-door policy.

Large Group Instruction

Poorly done, the large group aspect of team instruction could
bring disenchantment to both participants and observers. There are
mechanical details that may not be avoided without penalty. The
following suggestions are borrowed from *The Summer Institute in
Team Teaching,* Howard B. Mattlin Jr. High School, Plainview,
New York:

> . . . attention to the technical and mechanical details of a lesson
> is essential for successful large group instruction. Although
> seemingly so obvious, the following suggestions are included
> because they have not always been evident to teachers in pre-
> paring for large group lessons:
> *Seating.* The seating pattern should be arranged to expedite the
> desired kind of interaction between teacher, pupils, and ma-
> terials. A formal pattern seems appropriate when the flow of
> knowledge is from teacher, film, or machine toward the pupils.
> Those in the fringe areas ought to be able to see and hear at
> all times. When the roving mike is used for audience participa-
> tion, it is necessary to consider the aisle patterns. (Finally) the
> seating pattern should provide for the orderly flow of pupils
> during entrance and departure.
> *Collection and Distribution of Materials.* Special provisions
> should be made for efficient distribution and collection of mate-
> rials in large group instruction. Materials may be distributed
> to each seat prior to the lesson. Materials may be handed to

pupils upon entering and collected upon departure. Pupils may be trained to pick up materials on a table upon entrance and return same on departure.

Use and Display of Visual Materials. Materials and equipment should be ready ahead of time. Visual materials, whether they be maps, pictures, flannel-graph figures, posters, or writing on a chalkboard, should be of sufficient size and so located that all pupils can see.

Too many seemingly unrelated displays seem at times to be distracting to pupils.

The moving around of displays and materials during the lesson should be avoided.

The Lecture. Rhetorical questions should be avoided, as pupils from habit will raise hands and expect to answer. An alternate approach is, "I know if I asked this question, you would answer in this way . . ." Sharp focus is needed in lecturing. Organizing a presentation around clear, concise points, using a dramatic introduction, thorough development, and a final summarization seem a worthwhile procedure.

Other Groupings of Children

As noted previously, children may be deployed in an almost infinite variety of groupings. These will be dictated by the needs of the students, as defined by the team members, and will be limited only by availability of facilities and by other such practical considerations. Children may be left in homeroom groups, of course, or homeroom groups (or portions thereof) can be combined in large groups, or children may be exchanged between homeroom groups. During certain phases of instruction, it would not be unusual to find a large group (perhaps 60 children) working with one staff member, two or three smaller groups working under the direction of a second team member, individuals working independently in another classroom and only indirectly being supervised by a team member, and other individual pupils working independently in the library.

Utilization of Team Members

One important reason for the existence of the team is to most fully employ the special talents of each staff member. A team member who is particularly competent in mathematics may very well take leadership of the team during the course of a unit on mathematics. The teacher who is best able to develop small group and independent activities will probably take a leading role in the planning sessions in the selections of such activities. Whatever the special talent, it will be shared to a larger degree. In the sharing the members of the team are exposed to each other's strengths and this exposure may well enhance their overall instructional abilities.

Questions arise regarding procedure. Should all members of the staff be on hand when the large group lessons are being taught? Must we limit our groupings in recognition of the number of staff available?

Again, the specific situation dictates the course of action. It may be more profitable for two or three staff members to be engaged in planning activities while the large group lesson is in session. On the other hand, the nature of the lesson might require the presence of all.

Must we limit the number of sub-groups? This will depend on the availability of a substitute, the librarian, a teacher aide, or other specialized personnel. Nearby teacher colleges should be more than pleased to see their students getting experience as members of an instructional team.

A BLENDING: THE UNGRADED SCHOOL AND TEAM TEACHING

A natural partnership is able to exist between these two tools of education. Both promote individualization of instruction, the meeting of pupil needs based on the existing realities of the school situation.

After the decision for change has been made, after all the important preliminaries have been cared for (and there are many), it is recommended that the first step in the re-patterning of the elementary school be in the direction of ungrading. *The* vital person in education, the classroom teacher, must experience the freedom and the challenge of providing instruction geared to the very real children who exist in his classroom. A properly-implemented ungraded school does indeed place a formidible burden upon a teaching staff, a burden that only time, experience, and support (of administration and community) can ease.

As the philosophy of individualization becomes a way of life within the school, the time will have arrived for teachers to examine the profits to be derived from sharing. As the instructional leader of the school, the principal will provide the wherewithal for sharing, initiating the interim steps to the team approach. With time, the formal teams can be developed, and the blending will be achieved.

In this modern school, we can retain the attributes of the self-contained classroom; but as needs arise and are identified, we may bring into play the tools of the team approach. It may happen that all members of the school staff will be placed on teams and that the teams will always operate. This is unlikely. At least in the early period the teams will be used sporadically. It will be used most often when teacher aides, student teachers, and substitute teachers are easily available.

SUMMARY

Team teaching is another tool promoting the kind of flexibility that enables greater individualization of instruction and which capitalizes on teacher strengths through the dynamics of teaming. It deals creatively with the utilization of people, space, and time.

Before any formal plan of team teaching is adopted, it is recommended that certain interim steps be taken. These include intravisitations, and more simple forms of team planning and instruction. The main purpose of the preliminary steps is to prove the worth of the team idea, selling the notion to a staff in order to get a full measure of staff support.

Team teaching may take place throughout a building or it may involve a single team. The size of a team or the number of teams must depend on the specific needs of the building, the abilities of staff, and the degree of committment to the concept. The availability of extra clerical help and/or student teachers is a factor.

The ungraded school is a natural partner to the team idea. Each has the effect of meeting pupil needs by providing teachers with a wider assortment of means to more realistic objectives.

5

Specialists in the
Ungraded Schools

How may the practices of the librarian, the physical education instructor, the music teacher, and the art teacher contribute to the fulfillment of the ungraded school?

Enactment of the "tag-out," whereat the classroom teacher makes his exit from the classroom upon the entrance of the specialist, relegates the specialist to the role of relief-giver. But a school that prizes efficiency, which places value upon the notion of full and effective utilization of staff, is not able to tolerate the segregation that is implicit in such arrangement.

Elementary specialists need not be sub-class teachers. While directly giving instruction in their specialties, they can also give sustenance to specific classroom programs. Obviously, this is best accomplished through cooperative endeavor, teacher and specialist communicating. In planning together, in *working* together, the specialists' functions are enhanced, as is the overall school program.

OPERATION OF THE LIBRARY

How fully can a school library (and the librarian) benefit the school? The answer to this must be qualified. It depends on various factors: (1) the extensiveness of the book collection, (2) the physical lay-out of the library, (3) the availability of clerical assistance for the librarian, (4) the nature and scope of materials in the library, and (5) the library program, itself.

In order to most fully explore the potential riches of the library, we will examine the library program of the Central Park Road School of Plainview, Long Island. This elementary school received a substantial grant from the Knapp Foundation enabling it to meet the national standards for school libraries. It was one of two such schools selected in the nation (during Phase I of the library project) and, as such, it served as a demonstration center "to demonstrate the educational value of a full program of school library services."

With the aid of the grant received, the Central Park Road School, with a school population of 592 pupils (k-6), employed two full-time librarians and two part-time library aides. It added 600 new books to the children's collection bringing its total close to 6,000 books. Two hundred professional books were purchased; the number of magazine subscriptions was increased to eighty-four. Film-strips and records were added to the existing collections. This was indeed a realization of a librarian's dream. It was in fact the dream of the American Association of School Librarians. In dollar amount the grant exceeded $40,000.

What can happen when you have a highly desirable situation? Following were the expressed objectives of the program: [1]

Goals for Pupils
a) To teach children to use the school library effectively and efficiently in exploring the problems their teachers present.

---

[1] As found in *The Knapp School Libraries Project at Central Park Road School.* Plainview: Educational Communications Center, 1963.

b) To foster learning beyond the textbook in many subjects.
c) To encourage independent investigation in new or related areas.
d) To encourage the voluntary reading of worthwhile books which are appropriate to the child's growing level of maturity and reading skill.
e) To help each child to acquire a rich background of reading experience and, through various methods, to promote taste in reading and literary appreciation.
f) To promote the habit of using a library frequently—even daily.
g) To expose children to the operation and handling of media of all types in order to secure information.

Goals for Teachers
a) To show them individually and in groups how to use library materials most effectively.
b) To encourage greater utilization of resource materials in planning lessons.
c) To work cooperatively with librarians in the selection of materials related to the curriculum.
d) To make them acquainted with the content of some of the many useful and highly qualified children's books.
e) To improve instruction through the effective use of a variety of resource material found in the demonstration library.

Goals for Administrators
a) To demonstrate the kind of library program made possible when a budget provides for adequate personnel, library materials, and space as set forth in the *Standards for School Library Programs*.
b) To show a variety of ways in which library materials may be used for pleasure and educational growth, as well as for important tools of learning in the regular school curriculum.
c) To encourage close cooperation between the librarians, the teachers and the administration in planning and carrying out all areas of library service.

These are obviously worthy goals. What kind of program was put into effect which furthered the overall objectives?

Since Central Park Road School operated as a demonstration school, teachers and administrators achieved the goals set for them through exposure to the program, if outside the school, or through participation, if members of the demonstration school staff. The quality of their learning did, of course, hinge upon the quality of the program for the children.

Perhaps the most outstanding characteristics of the program that evolved, beyond the rich accumulation of materials, were its flexible scheduling and its frequent usage by the youngsters. An examination of the physical lay-out of the library (see illustration on page 117) clearly indicates the advantages of sufficient space.

With adjoining library rooms and two librarians, two classes were able to use the library simultaneously. The smaller of the rooms housed a selection of books and materials appropriate for the primary classes and the larger room was utilized for the pupils of the intermediate levels. There would be exceptions to this, depending upon specific situations.

Generally, teachers and their classes were able to use the facilities two or more times a week, depending upon need. Teachers, by signing up on the posted blank schedule each week, could reserve a particular day and time for the entire class. This time could be used for formal instruction in use of reference materials, for doing reference work, for group discussion and whole group activity, or for individual application of a taught research skill. Since the library housed tape recorders (and pre-recorded tapes), filmstrips, and records, children frequently made use of these learning materials.

Time was set aside each day for book exchange. Teachers sent their children for this activity as required by need rather than according to a set schedule. Thus, a child who was able to finish a book in one or two days was able to return it immediately thereafter, and then select another book if he so desired. Or, when a child found a book that he selected was unappealing, he exchanged it on the following day.

One very popular portion of the Central Park Road School pro-

FACILITIES (Two rooms)   1,840 Sq. Ft.

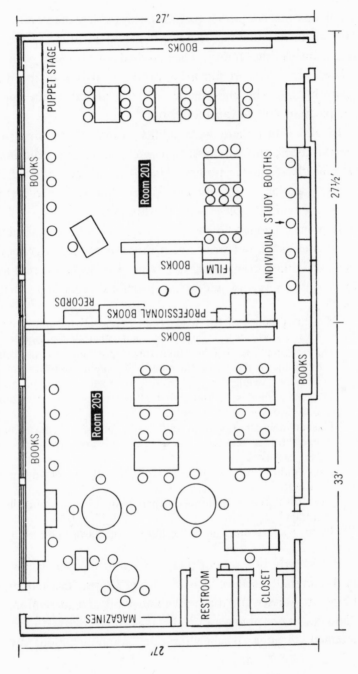

gram was the noon-time period during which time children could give up their half hour recreation period in order to spend additional time in the library. They studied, or browsed, or listened to records; they viewed filmstrips or slides in one of the individual study booths. The children treated this period as an opportunity for pleasant and rewarding leisure.

In all of this there were adults available: the librarians, the clerical aides, and the classroom teachers. Teachers did not simply deposit classes in the library. They participated with the librarian in the selection of activities, and they supervised the carrying out of the activities together with the librarian.

It is easy enough to carry out a good library program under ideal conditions, but what about those many, many schools where ideal conditions do not exist? Perhaps this question is best answered by posing a series of additional questions, regarding a School X:

> Is it the practice of the teachers of School X to simply deposit their classes in the library for their scheduled period?
> Do librarian and teacher take the opportunity to discuss the make-up of the class, the needs of specific pupils within the class, or teacher needs relating to certain class programs?
> Is there a rigid scheduling that allows entrance to the library only weekly or bi-weekly?
> Has anyone attempted to sell to the board of education the need for a relatively inexpensive library aide—even one for part-time?
> Are children ever permitted to use the library during periods of leisure?
> Are instructional materials other than books found in the library?
> Is the primary function of the library the act of book exchange?

Particularly in a school that adheres to the philosophy inherent in the ungraded school, it is important to gear the activities of the library to service for the individual pupil and to reinforce the individualization practices of the classroom teacher. This is best attained through teacher-librarian communication, by flexible scheduling, and, in general, by efficient and full usage of the resources of the library.

PHYSICAL EDUCATION IN THE UNGRADED SCHOOL

Questions were raised regarding the operation of the physical education classes at the Parkway School in the early phase of the ungraded program. The interage classes provoked greatest concern. Wouldn't the older children completely dominate, even physically endanger the younger children? How could the instructors cope with the vaster age range and its probably greater ability range?

There is no sound reason for the instructors of physical education to escape the need to treat the youngsters in their charge according to individual needs insofar as possible. Additionally, there is reason to believe that in many strictly graded classes, the ability range (in physical skills) is as great as and even greater than the ability range to be found in some ungraded inter-age classes. Conceivably, if we chose to design it so (although I can't imagine why), we could develop so-called interage classes where the age range might only be a month or two. Further, it may be argued that physical education instructors have had inter-age grouping in graded classes having retained children. Did this previously result in insurmountable crises?

The terrible spectre of older children belittling and bullying timid younger ones is a kind of exaggeration that is best dispelled by reference to real experience. Leonard Resnick, Parkway's physical education instructor at the writing of this book, developed a report dealing with the subject. The following excerpts are relevant:

> . . . the straight ungraded classes have not hindered or aided the organization of the physical education classes one iota. [Resnick refers to those which are not inter-age.] However, assuming that some of the children are placed with inter-age groups next year, it is especially helpful to keep records of skill

achievement in order to permit rapid skill groupings in the early part of the new school year. This additional record-keeping and the testing required are extra burdens, but it helps me to do my job better. . . . The interage groups are the classes that pose a few unique problems in the gym. The best way to cover the subject is to react to some of the activities that have been covered in these classes.

Mass Group Games. This is always the first unit I cover with the early primary children. The purpose is to teach them three or four games that can be played by large numbers indoors so that they will be actively and usefully engaged when indoors due to inclement weather during the noontime program. Some of the mass games taught were Circle Dodge Ball, 1-2-3, and Beanbag Toss.

These activities were *vastly aided* by the mixed age groupings, since most of the children already played the game and knew exactly what was expected of them. The children who never played these games followed their lead and played the game with fewer spot corrections by me.

In Dodge Ball, some of the bigger children and harder throwers dominated the game, but domination by a few in this type of game is usually the case, even in straight age pairings. This is helped somewhat by having more than one circle and by close instructor supervision.

Relay Races. In relay races, the interage grouping posed no major problem. In some instances a minor adjustment had to be made so that the relay used was not too difficult in terms of manual dexterity required.

Scooter Activities and Games. Working up the sequence, from scooter positions to scooter relay races to scooter games was very simple. Of course, for some it was review. They enjoyed it particularly for they could demonstrate to the newcomers.

Stunts and Tumbling. Tumbling lends itself ideally to the interage groups. In this type of unit, skill rather than chronological age is the ideal way to group. The classes were tested on basics (log roll, forward roll) and then placed in groups according to degree of skill. The children were moved up or down into other groups as they formed their skills. I worked with one group while the others were practicing a given stunt. Age lines are crossed frequently in this activity.

In Summary. The interage groupings make me more aware of

the need to consider individual differences. I need to more carefully select activities, to divide groups within groups for maximum efficiency. It results in refinement of skill groupings.
I find I must be more explicit in my directions. Since the attention span is greatly varied, the demands on me by the children
seem to have increased measurably. They sometimes appear
to be vying for my attention.

If Resnick's report is to be taken as a serious and carefully
considered evaluation of his experience with the ungraded school
(and I do take it seriously), and if this evaluation is a barometer
of what can be expected with interage groupings, then we may
smile patronizingly at the alarm-ringers . . . and ignore them.
Physical education is not a thing apart from the demands of the
ungraded school. It faces those demands. The highly competent
instructor becomes "more aware of the need to consider individual
differences" and will "more carefully select activities, dividing
groups within groups for maximum efficiency, resulting in refinement of skill groupings."

To place greater stress on the positive aspects of inter-age
grouping in physical education, additional mention must be
made of the immense improvement in instructional efficiency that
results when *all* children are *not* at the same point of instruction,
when a substantial number of children are used to teach their less
experienced schoolmates. Another example of this is found in the
teaching of the unit on square dancing. The number of hours
required to teach the basic steps to first year students was actually
cut in half as a result of having second year students assisting
through example and participation.

The same procedure, carried into the intermediate section, produces similar results in all areas of skill instruction. Experience
tells us that inter-age classes ought not to be considered an evil
to be tolerated in physical education, but rather another desirable
feature, promoting increased teacher efficiency.

GENERAL MUSIC IN THE UNGRADED SCHOOL

The program of general music in the elementary school usually calls for group singing, music appreciation, some active participation in rhythm exercises, learning to play simple pieces on the flutophone (as an introduction to an instrumental program), and basics of note-reading. This would be true in graded or ungraded schools.

The most effective teacher of general music is aware of differences of ability within each of the classrooms served and plans his program accordingly. The especially talented child is challenged. Those talents are displayed during the formal presentation of the chorus, the flutophone band, and by the band and orchestra when these are a part of the music program. The less talented are provided with a general exposure and with a sequentially developed series of basic skills.

As with regular academic classroom activities there are innumerable opportunities for whole class lessons. The "danger" of repetition in the interage classes is easily averted, simply through teacher awareness of the danger and accompanying proper long-range planning. Songs taught one year need not be taught the succeeding year since there are in existence large numbers of appropriate selections. A two or three year cycling system can be put into effect. The same can be done with music appreciation.

In formal instruction, particularly in note-reading, there is a need to know what has already been achieved by the individual pupil. The teacher discovers this through testing, or through having kept records of mastery, but probably through a combination of the two. This, of course, should result in differentiation of instruction within the classroom. Yet, though possibly to a lesser degree, the same should be true in the "straight grade."

It has been made clearly evident that the physical education program and *all* instructional programs are made more efficient through the development of teacher sensitivity to the need for plans geared to the *real* children existing within each classroom. We can include the music program. The myth of the average child—who has never existed—must suffer the fate of the ice box and the kerosene lamp. They have a certain historical value, but are otherwise quaint anachronisms.

ART IN THE UNGRADED SCHOOL

Most dramatically, through the violence of color and design, the individuality of the pupil finds expression. Creativity, a prize unto itself, is closely related to individuality. Which art teacher would make himself a leveler, demanding conformity and the mass-produced look? Let me hope, for all of us, there will be no affirmative response to that question.

It is conceivable that the art teacher can develop one class within the building with the largest possible age range and still conduct a successful lesson. Whether clay or crayon, paint or paper and paste, these fit into the smallest and largest of hands.

That there are *levels* of proficiency cannot be denied; however, once again, no perceptive teacher would argue that all children move from level to level at a predictable and even rate. Accepting the truth of unpredictability, it then requires a teacher and a curriculum to accommodate the prized individuality.

The art curriculum of Central School District Four recognizes three general stages of growth (in art) in the elementary school; these are described in broad categorizations as follows:

Manipulative Stage. (ages 4—7) In this stage the child is introduced to art materials for exploration through manipulation, primarily. He establishes a relationship to the materials based on how he is able to use the materials to express his feelings about the world (wherein he is the center). Colors, shapes, and forms relate in size and intensity according to the way the child feels about particular things. (At this stage, especially, psychologists are able to learn a great deal about a child's inner workings through his art expression.) Growth in art ability can be noted as the child (1) gives greater attention to detail, (2) shows confidence in all art activity, (3) demonstrates freedom from stereotyped repetitions, and (4) indicates awareness of particular environments.

Symbolic Stage. (ages 7—10) Types of symbols that have been developed by the child result from his own knowledge and personality, and these might include the following: a concept of the human figure, a relation of color to objects, a basic space relationship of earth to sky, and a use of geometric shapes and lines to represent concepts.

Deviations from symbolic representation result when the child becomes experientally involved with the activity; that is, the human figure may be exaggerated according to importance to him, or two things might be happening at different times in the same picture . . . and such.

Growth at this stage of development is seen as: (1) the child's concepts are clearly expressed, (2) textures of objects become important, (3) complex space relationships come into use—beyond the basic earth-sky approach, (4) color to object relations come into being, and (5) the subject matter of art varies greatly.

Cognizant Stage. (ages 10—13) In moving from childhood toward the teen-age years, the youngster begins to feel social concerns. He becomes a conformist to peer standards; but he also tends to choose to represent things as they really are, emphasizing the details of his representations.

Growth in this stage will be seen, not only in how accurately the pupil makes his representations, but through the pupil's ability to sustain individual creativity.

It can be seen that this generalized description of a child's stages of development in art not only does not dictate restrictions because of age, but rather demands that no two pupils be encouraged to be do-alikes.

If art is held to be the antithesis of indistinguishable sameness, a defender of individuality, then it is in proper company when it exists in the ungraded school. In such an environment, it should blossom most strongly.

What specific materials are required and what specific procedures and program can be developed for art in the ungraded school? The answers must be determined locally. They are dependent upon the extent of the art budget, the art teacher's pupil load as well as upon teacher skill and ingenuity. To qualify as "ungraded," the art program need only seek out means of developing art attitudes and skills in pupils based upon individual needs and abilities. The art teacher who believes this will find no problems in the interage class that are not problems in classes in general. Along these lines, quality of program hinges upon the teacher's knowledge of each child.

This may be a side issue, but it is worthy of note. I have been advised by classroom teachers and by art teachers alike that the social aspect of the interage barrier is hurdled first and most easily through the art program. The older children in the class are most apt to be interested in the resultant product of the younger child, to the point of expressing big-brother approval and encouragement; in some instances, it is acceptance on the level of equals.

THE IMPORTANCE OF FLEXIBLE SCHEDULING

I discussed flexible scheduling in describing an effective library program. Anything other than flexible scheduling in the special areas serves to interfere with the administrative freedom that ought to be characteristic of the ungraded school.

The common practice, in those elementary schools fortunate enough to have the services of the special teachers, is to develop a schedule in each of the special areas at the beginning of the year. These are adhered to throughout the year. Thus, a teacher may have art for his class every Tuesday at 10 A.M. for forty minutes, fifty minutes of physical education every Thursday at 2 P.M., etc.

Consider the disadvantages. There may well be times when the art lesson would be most successful if the art teacher could remain with the class for 90 minutes instead of the 40, or it might only require the specialist's direct attention for 20 minutes. How many skills are left untaught simply because the alloted time prohibits their introduction? How frequently does the specialist find himself stretching a lesson simply to fill in the time that has been assigned?

I would hope that the majority of elementary teachers have the freedom to exercise their judgments regarding the amount of time devoted to daily lessons. When the science lesson comes to a happy conclusion at the end of 35 minutes, it would seem pathetically foolish to squeeze out another ten minutes because a piece of paper from on high demands that the science lesson must be 45 minutes in length. Pieces of paper were not meant to be our masters.

If it is obviously right that the teacher in the self-contained classroom be allowed to utilize professional judgment, then it should be equally true for the specialist. Is it so difficult to manage flexibility?

Practice in the art of flexible scheduling develops proficiency in the users. Initially, for some, the task is overwhelming. Proper attitude, coupled with a reasonable degree of enthusiasm, will produce success.

After agreement is reached that the specialists will use flexible scheduling, the procedure might be to have one of the group develop his program—the physical education instructor, for example. The time slots would be placed on a master schedule and would show blocks of time for certain groups of classes (Tuesday: 9:00 - 11:00, fourth year students; Wednesday: 9:00 - 10:00, interage classes—1st and second year students). The second specialist to tackle the schedule would seek to respect those time designations in setting up his schedule. If a conflict seemed probable, he would sit with specialist no. 1 and iron out the problem. This accomplished, specialist no. 3 comes upon the scene and, with more difficulty, develops his schedule. All of these would be developing *blocks of time* for certain groups of classes, as opposed to giving specific minute allotments per single class. By using blocks of time, the instructor alows himself the leeway of providing a larger package of time for one class within the block, with somewhat smaller shares for the others within the block. However, on the following week, a different time package would be given. At year's end, it is probable that the amount per class would have evened itself out.

Once the conflicts are scheduled out, the team of specialists are able to work in relative independence. In practice, however, specialists find themselves borrowing from each others' packages of time throughout the year.

There is a sacrifice required for the flexibility gained. Since a new specific schedule comes into existence each week, the specialist must be given a period of time at the end of each week in which to develop the new weekly schedule. For efficiency's sake, it is desirable to have the specialists work these out in the same room, not necessarily communicating with each other, but together in the event that some communication is necessary.

The effectiveness of flexible scheduling does not rest entirely upon the shoulders of the specialists. There may be instances when certain of the classroom teachers will resist the concept. It is less troublesome to have a regularly scheduled period each week, one that can be counted on, and which will not require that the classroom teacher play a role in determining the schedule. In flexible scheduling the classroom teacher is expected to ask for longer or shorter periods, to request specific assistance for a classroom project that relates to the specialist's skills. When he does not, then the specialist makes the determination . . . and it may not be to the liking of the classroom teacher.

It cannot be denied that flexible scheduling does demand more effort and more time from specialist and from classroom teacher, and it requires that the building principal give support and attention to the idea. The principal, initially, and for the first few weeks of operation, should carefully note the progress of the scheduling.

Are there, in fact, variations in the schedule based on expressed needs? Or, out of resistance, has it fallen into the patterns of rigid scheduling? It is difficult to get real profit from the idea when the specialist rejects the notion. When a specialist demonstrates his apathy or outright resistance, it is wise to acquiesce to reality and to permit additional clinging to the preferred method . . . temporarily. It is possible to have one teacher rigidly scheduling, while the others are not. Time, peer pressure, and gentle prodding will eventually bring about unanimity.

SUMMARY

Specialists are not apart from the ungraded school. They must contribute to the program inasmuch as the philosophy of the ungraded school is meant to pervade every aspect of the school.

In providing for *each* pupil—to the extent possible—the specialist discovers it essential to keep clearer, more specific records on each child. The interage feature of the ungraded plan need not handicap any of the specialists. In the area of physical education, the instructor finds it especially necessary to plan always in light of the real make-up of the class, as opposed to the idea of planning for a grade level. This must be the experience of each of the specialists.

As with the classroom teacher, the specialist learns that the ungraded program is more demanding, in effort and in time. Teacher knowledge of the pupil must go beyond the superficial. Planning is more complex. Rewards, it is hoped, would be greater, also.

Since the ungraded school features flexibility, the specialist, as an important part of the teaching team, ought to develop his schedules in order to foster that flexibility, allowing varying periods of time for the classroom. Time allotment, which can change weekly, would stem from actual need.

6

Self-Study: A Prelude to Change

The agriculturist evaluates soil, climate, and general environmental conditions in seeking to determine the likelihood of sustaining life for a certain species of plant in a particular area. In like manner, through careful examination, it is possible to anticipate the chances for a successful implementation of the ungraded school in a particular school district. After the strengths and the needs of a school have been examined, a plan of action is not far away.

All aspects of the existing school setting should be probed, but most particularly the school philosophy, the statement of goals, the curriculum, the attitudes of staff and administration regarding the proposed changes, and the receptiveness of the board of education and the community in general. To neglect certain of these steps is conceivable. Programs may be put into operation when none of the preliminary work is done. The risk, however, proportionately increases with step-skipping. Even with the greatest of preparation, the introduction of a major educational innovation is a somewhat hazardous undertaking. The dangers are multiplied when the groundwork is poorly laid.

It has happened, more than once, that one person assumed almost complete responsibility for initiating the ungraded program in his school or school district. Insufficient broad support or enthusiasm was mustered. The one-man operation collapsed—was discontinued—when the individual left the district. In other situations, discontinuance was brought about by a failure to clarify the responsibilities of each segment of the educational team, including central administration, the board, and the community.

THE STATEMENT OF PHILOSOPHY

A statement of philosophy is the most important document to be found in a school district. Not unlike our basic political documents (the Constitution, the Bill of Rights), it serves as the framework within which we must operate if we are to be true to ourselves. A school district philosophy unites its professional staff through the identification of its loftier goals, giving common direction and purpose.

That philosophy which is a group of words put together by someone at some time in the past and which is filed "somewhere" is obviously of little value, if it has value at all. As badly off, in this respect, are those districts which have failed to take the time for the development of written expression of philosophy.

There may be the "inbetweeners," of course, who have in existence a reasonably good statement, perhaps only in need of some modification, followed by a re-publishing. Whatever the case, the originating or the revival of an expressed philosophy is a good starting-off point in the process of self-examination.

The words that are finally strung together should be, in fact, a genuine reflection of the philosophy of those individuals, administrators and teachers, entrusted with putting into effect the school curriculum. This is best accomplished when there is involvement on a broad scale in the development of the document. Lay participation by key citizens, those particularly who are concerned with quality education, may be beneficial. Acceptance, approval, and formal adoption of education adds a kind of final authority and begets a commitment of value from this ultimately influential group.

Educational goals are very much related to philosophy, as borne out by this statement excerpted from the Department of Elementary Principals' yearbook of 1961:

> ... If a group subscribes to a philosophy which supports a sitting-listening-memorizing-reciting kind of education, or holds to a philosophy which maintains that every child should be exposed as much as possible to every "important" subject, then the goals will reflect these beliefs. On the other hand, if a group subscribes to a philosophy which supports the point of view that learning is a gradual process of growth in each individual, goals will reflect this particular point of view . . . each philosophy will be associated with particular kinds of behavioral outcomes as goals.[1]

Once a philosophy exists, every act of education may be measured against it. Is there conflict or agreement? New ideas, new programs will tend to support the philosophy or face rejection because they do not. In appraising curricula, even supervisory practices, the main point of reference may well be the expression of philosophy that has been formally adopted. What better purpose could it serve?

As an example of a document which has especially influenced the direction of education within a community, the statement of the philosophy of the Plainview-Old Bethpage School District is

---

[1] National Education Association, *Elementary School Organization, Purposes, Patterns, Perspectives.* Washington, D.C.: NEA Department of Elementary School Principals, 1961. p.8.

reproduced (see p. 133). Note particularly how certain sections mandate the development of educational programs tailored to the individual pupil:

> ... and must educate all of our children, the bright, the aver-
> age, and the slow learning.
> ... The modern school must be built on the precept that no
> two children are alike in ability or personality traits. No single
> standard of achievement can be set for all pupils and each must
> be challenged to work to his greatest capacity. Each child must
> be regarded as a separate, important individual, etc.

Does the above support best the objectives of the graded or the ungraded school? Obviously, the Plainview-Old Bethpage statement of philosophy dictated a course of educational action that pulled it forcefully from the ranks of districts plodding along in the fashion of "the good old days." Accorded a leading role, the philosophy provided direction, serving as a prod for constant evaluation and improvement.

It is noteworthy that at one point in the history of the district a New York University survey team severely criticized the district's lack of educational coordination and its undifferentiated instructional practices. The chapter of the report dealing with elementary education had this to say about the problems of "sameness":

> ... The goals of accomplishment for each grade need to be re-
> considered and revised in the light of what we know about
> individual growth and learning. In classrooms there is too much
> —much too much—sameness. Too many children read the
> *same* reader, the *same* science book, use the *same* workbooks.
> Research tells us that in a typical first grade the range of
> achievement is four to five years and that by the time children
> reach the sixth grade the range is eight to nine years. Yet, in
> each grade we find this sameness ... schools must do far better
> than they are now doing to offer a program suited to each indi-
> vidual.[2]

---

[2] New York University. *Education for Today and Tomorrow*. New York: Center for School Services, School of Education, New York University, 1957. p. 32.

Following the survey, there resulted an ongoing program of self-evaluation and the development of philosophy and goals. In 1964, seven short years after the damning report of the survey team, Plainview-Old Bethpage was cited by the United States Office of Education as a district which was especially able to successfully incorporate desirable innovations, one of three districts on the eastern seaboard so distinguished.[3]

GENERAL STATEMENT OF PLAINVIEW—OLD BETHPAGE EDUCATIONAL PHILOSOPHY

Our democratically-organized schools should provide a desirable environment where the children of all the people are given countless opportunities to grow at their own rate in their individual way — physically, emotionally, mentally, and socially.

"Democratically-organized" — Our schools must be based on the assumption that, in the democratic tradition, pupils, staff members, school board representatives, and the public have certain rights, not the least of which is to share in the development of matters that affect each group. However, with rights come responsibilities, not the least of which is to follow policies and regulations established by those authorities who have the legal or professional responsibility for so doing.

"Where the children of all the people"—In America, our public schools are not restricted in any sense. Plainview-Old Bethpage schools are truly the people's schools and the only social agency that has contact with all the future citizens of our country. Such schools then, must be geared to take care of a tremendous assortment of children from many different cultural and economic backgrounds, and must educate all of our children, the bright, the average, and the slow-learning.

"Countless opportunities"—Our children have a right to expect that an interested citizenry will provide them with the best schools, teachers, and items of instruction that can be afforded. Once these facilities and personnel are provided, they should be efficiently utilized to furnish the children with learning experiences of many valuable varieties.

---

[3] The System Development Corporation of Santa Monica, Calif., under contract with the U.S. Office of Education, undertook the project of "exploring the dynamic processes of educational change." The other eastern districts selected for this project were: Manhasset, N.Y., and Newton, Mass.

"Grow at their own rate in their individual way"—The modern school must be built on the precept that no two children are alike in ability or personal traits. No single standard of achievement can be set up for all pupils and each must be challenged to work to his greatest capacity. Each child must be regarded as a separate, important individual with instruction and learning situations geared to provide success through effort, for children at all levels. Every provision for individual differences must be made, and this requires class sizes small enough to be handled efficiently.

"Physically, emotionally, mentally, and socially"—The development and growth of the whole child must be a primary objective of our schools. To develop the mental aspect of the child without consideration for the other vital factors in the total growth pattern is insufficient. It is the job of our public schools to see that the child grows in all ways and school experiences should be planned accordingly.

THE STATEMENT OF GOALS

Through a statement of general goals, a district focuses on what it ought to do for its young people. These goals must obviously be related to the expressed philosophy, elaborating on the sentiments found therein. Additionally, the goals ought to be realistic in terms of local conditions, including needs and aspirations.

A community undergoing self-examination will find value in taking into account what it expects to achieve, what it would like to achieve for the young people in its care. Goals defined are good intentions. As such, they are able to stimulate the doers (the classroom teachers), inspiring the kind of activity that will bring the goals to fruition . . . or those written goals may suffer the humiliating imprisonment that befalls the many pieces of paper that are sentenced to life within the maze of the filing cabinet, perhaps under the heading, *Deeds Undone*. It is apparent that the value of this basic document is dependent upon the quality of effort that brought it into existence . . . and the ensuing use of it.

In relation to the ungraded program, the statement of goals definitely must contain expressions that may be pointed to as supportive of the ungraded philosophy. Statements might be included that emphasize the need to provide youngsters with opportunities to develop their special abilities or which underline the obligations of the school to provide individual guidance. To focus on the individual student is to declare allegiance to the kind of thinking that promotes the ungraded school.

THE STUDY OF ATTITUDES

Primary Staff

However desirable an idea, its value is wholly dependent upon those individuals entrusted with the task of breathing life into it. Any program that is inflicted upon an unwilling, antagonistic teaching staff will be labeled "gimmick" and, as such, will receive irreverent treatment. Success under such unfavorable circumstances is beyond even hope.

How may we determine that a need exists for change? When staff acknowledges this need, and if they are given a role in bringing it about, the chances for success are handsomely multiplied.

In the Plainview-Old Bethpage School District, previous to talking loudly about the merits of the ungraded school, a teacher-attitude survey was developed locally. It was constructed so as not to include specific reference to the ungraded school. The purpose of the survey was to determine whether or not the primary teachers were apt to be receptive to the notion of the ungraded school. To promote response untainted by the desire to please administration, the teachers were asked not to sign their responses.

Five items were chosen, concerned with (1) retention, (2) acceleration, (3) individual and small group instruction, (4) the matter of primary children's physical and mental maturity, and (5) teacher attitude about seeking solution to the problems of the primary school. Teachers were asked to react with "yes" or "no" and to add comments if desired. The questionnaires were distributed to all of the one hundred and fifteen primary teachers.

One hundred responses were received. Only four answered with checkmarks alone and without comment. Perhaps because the survey was particularly short, many teachers responded almost effusively with comments.

The first two questions, on retention and acceleration, were constructed as follows:

1. In your opinion, is retention a device that should be used with greater frequency in order to maintain minimum educational standards?

          _____Yes   _____No

Comments:_____

2. Is acceleration a device that dictates to the best interests of the rapid learner?

          _____Yes   _____No

Comments:_____

Fifty-eight percent of the teachers indicated flatly that they did not believe that retention would resolve the problem of the slower learning child. Of those that called for greater use of retention, many commented that their responses were prompted by their reluctance to place children in situations of continuous failure. Others said that retention should be used "only when it will benefit the child to remain in the same grade for a second year."

One teacher suggested that "having a nongraded primary school might handle this problem." Another responded that "A good educational system should have a continuous flow of learning. Why is retention necessary? Children should be properly grouped and placed so that retention is not necessary."

How comforting it was to know that, from among the staff, there existed two very staunch allies, whose loyalty was unsolicited. Additionally, it was pleasing to see that most of the staff were not in favor of retention as a device for dealing with the slow-learning child. Even the advocates qualified their vote with expressions of concern for their children.

Sixty-eight percent of the teachers felt that acceleration was not a desirable means of coping with the rapid learner. In their comments they expressed the belief that those children could be given enrichment, or "more challenging material" to satisfy their appetites for learning.

The third question of the survey dealt with teacher attitude on the matter of individual and small group instruction. A negative response might well indicate that the staff felt uncomfortable with this manner of instruction, or that they were not convinced of its merits. The question:

3. Individual and small group instruction requires extensive planning. On the basis of results observed and as a matter of opinion, are you prepared to say that the efforts expended will produce desirable educational results?

    _____Yes   _____No

Comments:_____

Seventy-four percent of the staff gave a definitely affirmative response, while only fourteen percent gave a flat "no." The remaining twelve percent were qualified. They suggested that "smaller classes are needed" or that "we ought to use better grouping to control the wide ranges."

The obvious appreciation of the need for individual and small group instruction was reassuring. Ungrading would really not be a startling change for this kind of staff.

The last two questions dealt with the matter of range in the physical and particularly the mental development of primary children.

4. Is the matter of range in the physical and mental maturity of primary children a major problem?

_____ Yes   _____ No

Comments:_____

5. Do you feel that the problem noted in Item 4, above, is worthy of special study?

_____ Yes   _____ No

Comments:_____

Eighty percent of the staff indicated that this was a major problem. Sixteen percent did not agree, while the remaining four percent gave qualified answers, to the effect that this was a problem, but one that would always be with us.

Seventy-four percent of the teachers felt that a special study would be helpful. Most "no" answers were without expressed reason, although there was reason to believe that there was a reluctance to devote effort in another district study.

In summary, these were the responses:

1. Most teachers did not believe in retention or acceleration as good devices for coping with instructional problems. Comments about "flow of education" showed a high degree of teacher sophistication, and of the kind necessary for initiating an ungraded program.

2. Teachers felt the necessity for gearing instruction to individuals and small groups.

3. Teachers recognized the range of physical and mental abilities in primary children as a matter of major concern and believed the problem worthy of study.

On the basis of the survey results, we knew that the primary staff of Plainview-Old Bethpage would welcome rather than resist the idea of the ungraded plan.

And what should happen in the community where the staff demonstrates a more negative attitude? In a plan of continuous progress we take the pupil from where he is to as far as he is able to go. The same rule must apply for the teaching staff. District in-service courses and day-by-day supervision may be used as instruments to propagandize, if we find the concept desirable enough.

An excellent means of filling the teaching ranks with a staff likely to support the program is in our recruitment and hiring. Aggressive recruitment and a good interview are worth the effort.

It is only a guess, but I suspect that there are many schools where tenure is almost an automatic procedure, except in the rarest of cases. The poor teachers who stay on as a result will in no way help in getting a program started. After it is started, if it is, the poor teacher will be pointed to constantly as proof that "it doesn't work."

Building administration

If eventually a program is going to be adopted on a district-wide basis (where there is more than one elementary building), then we will find ourselves in need of determining administrator attitude. Are they blissful about the educational program as it exists? Are they able to cast a critical eye to the point of action?

It is within the power of the chief school administrator to encourage an organized program of self-analysis leading to desirable educational departures. Assuming that administrator No. 1 does support a plan of inquiry, it is his responsibility to give real evidence of that support. He must do this in words and deeds, through providing the moving force or forces for change, with opportunities for presentations to the full administrative group. He himself must become especially familiar with the implications of the proposed new concept and must make his office available for the resolution of those problems of implementation arising in the early stages.

One does not provoke excitement and enthusiasm in a school superintendent by casually suggesting a radical innovation for the district. Pressures from every direction are everlastingly exerted on him in efforts to command his influence. The gentle but firm brush-off becomes a technique of survival for the superintendent. A positive response is most likely when the propositions made are solidly founded, when he is furnished with the most clearly descernible rationale. From experience, the chief school administrator is aware of the need to expect arguments against those propositions which individuals make arguments for. Those who anticipate *his* needs, and who meet them successfully, will win his essential support.

Through opportunities provided by the superintendent, the proponents of the ungraded school will make known their proposals. To reduce the possibility of associating ideas with personalities, a team presentation is best. The team might consist of a building principal, a reading specialist, a primary teacher, and a psychologist. All of these would find value in the concept from the points of view they ordinarily represent.

At the time of presentation, assuming that the building administrators participated in discussion of the ideas, the attitudes of these key people would become known. The scope of the undertaking might well lead to—ought to lead to—a series of meetings, in the sense of in-service training. In this way the thinking of administration may be directed, not in the sense of brain-washing, but through the persuasiveness of logic. If the logic is good, successful persuasion is the outcome. As is true with teachers, the support of these professionals is essential in effecting the kind of change which is for the good of the district.

Community

Perhaps the easiest way of determining the prevailing attitude of the community-at-large is to check the number of ayes and nays of the latest budget vote. Like it or not, most school communities are very dollar-conscious. If the sole contact with the schools begins and ends at the voting lever, a measurable change in school practice may well meet with taxpayer resistance.

Yet, whatever the correlation between vote and attitude, it is best to use a variety of gauges to measure taxpayer mood. A well-organized parent-teacher organization can be used to advantage. As with teaching staff, the questionnaire may be used to advantage. In addition to revealing public opinion, it may stimulate public thought on educational matters.

In New York State, the state's educational forces do make available survey teams whose responsibilities include delving into attitudes and practices of local schools. They also provide the means for exploring samplings of taxpayer feelings about schools. The particular advantage of using an outside agency is in the objectivity it allows. Their recommendations also serve to reinforce a drive for educational improvement.

A LOOK AT CURRICULUM

In many communities, the curriculum turns out to be the textbooks that have been selected for the schools. In others, there is a careful spelling out of material to be covered on a grade level basis . . . even to the point of specifying the page numbers to be completed by certain dates. This is not exaggeration, for I have seen them. On the topic of rigidity: it was my own experience as a teacher of science in a departmentalized elementary school to be mildly reprimanded by a visiting superintendent for not filling out the full forty-five minutes of the science period. I had ended quite gracefully after forty-one minutes. Happily, the window shades were evenly set down.

The main question of investigation: is the existing curriculum able to yield to the theory and practice of the ungraded school?

In most, in nearly *all* instances, the textbooks on the market are rigidly structured according to the grade concept. When curriculum is left exclusively to the mercy of the textbook publishers, the implementation of the concept is severely handicapped. The teacher who relies entirely on the textbook writer has little need to think for himself. Certainly he has little opportunity to exercise his own ingenuity or to demonstrate concern for his pupils' special strengths or shortcomings, if he is a true partner in that unholy marriage of textbook and teacher.

Has it ever happened that a child in an intermediate grade has been unable even mechanically to read his social studies and science assignments? It would be more comfortable for us not to venture a guess regarding the scope of this educational crime. Lately, expressions of concern are published about the other end of the scale, where we find youngsters bored to the point of dismay because of exposure to unchallenging material, although it is the material of the grade level and contained in the textbook selected for that level. The good teacher knows that this is not necessary. Yet, without supporting curriculum, and materials, the individualized program is no easy task. Unbelieveable as it may seem, the teacher who attempts to overcome the imposed limitations may even be courting allegations of incompetence, or insubordination. It is the road to nowhere that is traveled most cozily·

The day may come, soon we hope, when it will be common practice for the textbook publishers to produce materials covering the same general information at more than one level of difficulty. Also, instead of year-sized books, publishers may develop them in smaller units. Thus, the ungraded schools themselves may determine the amount of material to be covered during the course of the year. These may be more or less than "average" and will be dependent upon the class make-up. This sort of practice will allow schools to adopt a multi-basal approach without the expense now entailed.

When the curriculum is developed locally and is not entirely dependent on the textbooks in use, is there provision for those other than the average pupil? Is it geared horizontally, according to grade level? A school that expects to go ungraded will either be forced to discard such a program, or modify it. Otherwise it will be another instance of ungradedness more in name than in fact.

A LOOK AT THE REPORTING SYSTEM

The idea of the grade (grade one, grade two, etc.) is hammered into parents and students when the reporting system encourages statements about "below grade level," "at grade level," or even "above grade level." Such reporting gives support to the mythical nonesuch, *the grade level,* the elusive abominable creation in the world of school children. It is a contradiction to the philosophy of the ungraded school and, as such, cannot be tolerated in the ungraded school.

Educators universally bemoan the evils and the shortcomings of the reporting systems that have been all too common, the A, B, C, D, and F, or the E, G, C, D, and F . . . or some other symbol system. All of these are a kind of shorthand, highly susceptible to misinterpretation by the parents. Time and again it has been proved, at the various levels of public and private education, that an *A* to one teacher is a *B* to another and, in some instances, may be a *C* or *D* to still another. This being true, how can we expect the parent to grasp the full meaning of the coded language to be found in that abused, confused, and confounding written report?

Has it not also been true that some parents, far too many parents, have paid children for the grades received? Depending upon degree of home affluence, the *A* is worth so much while a *B* is worth some lesser amount; or else the monetary value of the report is based upon improvement. At one point even the supermarkets got into the act, actually giving stamps (green, I think) for those desirable *A*'s. Children can hardly be blamed for suspecting that the real purpose of school is to get good marks. The act of learning becomes incidental.

Has it ever been true that a teacher has reduced a mark, or threatened to reduce an academic mark because of misconduct, or because a homework assignment was not done, or not completed? Perhaps a sloppy paper, despite the quality and accuracy of content, was graded low because of sloppiness? In all of this the mark is not a true reflection of the child's learning, but is rather a reward or a punishment. It becomes a weapon for inducing conformity, the supreme goal in the foolish section of our society. Amusingly enough, the Teachers' Colleges, which should know better, retain the symbol system of reporting.

Ungraded elementary schools have faced the need to extract themselves from the silliness of symbols. In general, they have taken to anecdotal reporting, reinforced by formal and frequent informal parent-teacher conferences. Progress in terms of specific activities is discussed, or recorded in written form. (See Appendix A, section dealing with reporting.)

Anecdotal reporting, doing away with the need for translation, reducing the probability of misinterpretation, usually provides the greatest amount of information for the parent . . . which is the real function of the progress report. However, *anecdotal reporting requires that the teacher take the time to meditate for unusually long periods about each of his students.* This is *not* a disadvantage, except that it is bound to be tiring, more time-consuming. The number of written reports should be fewer in number if these are to replace the simpler symbol reports.

Skill in the actual phrasing of the essay-type report develops with practice. Teachers will profit from parent reaction to their reports, and from sharing ideas with each other. Administration, by setting guidelines, by attentive examination of the written comments, are able to induce the desired quality.

Following are excerpts from a communication to the teachers of Parkway School, from the principal, related to the matter of reporting:

The report card should be thought of as an additional means of describing each child's school progress to parents. Its success will hinge in large part on the previous contacts you have had with those same parents, on their appreciation of school program and goals, and on their understanding of the general principles of child growth.

Our cards avoid symbolization. Symbols alone, in their simplicity, are too easily misunderstood, raise more questions than are answered, and therefore fail in their intended function.

Our use of comments was intended to overcome the proved weaknesses of the naked symbols. Obviously, poorly phrased comments will do no better for us and can even more elaborately confuse our communication. From experience we ought to develop certain generalizations, some do's and don't's to steer us towards our real goal and away from the pitfalls.

Not unlike the youngsters in our charge, we are entitled to our own "individual differences." Comments here are not intended to strangle your initiative, nor put to test your own creativity. Moreover, it would not be at all improper for you to share with your colleagues those ideas on reporting which you have found to be worthwhile.

In a few instances, it is conceivable that we would know enough about the parent (through previous contact) to enable us to use phrasing that we are certain would be appropriate for their understanding.

Some Cautions

Never
The report card is never to be used as an instrument for punishment. Such use thoroughly discredits the mis-users and effectively destroys communication.

Try Hard
It is difficult to advise parents that performance is poor, that conduct is bad. The difficulty is made complex by other factors, such as the fact that a child is performing at maximum, or when the child's behavior borders on emotional disturbance and seems beyond his control. In the extreme cases, this calls for a face-to-face conference (which should be requested on the card). In less than extreme cases, it is difficult but possible to be honest without appearing offensive. Nor is this a call for mumbo-jumbo. Search for an appropriate phrase. Ask a colleague, including our assistant principal or myself. Honesty, in the long run, serves us all best.

Really!
Not extraneous verbiage, nor redundancy, nor super-quantity is desirable. The goal is to make ourselves understood, to report pupil progress, without denying information.

When an elementary school becomes ungraded, it is the usual practice to identify for the parents their child's specific level of achievement in reading (at least) at the time of the report. Then comments relative to the specific level are made.

Parent-Teacher Conferences

Those communities that go into the parent-teacher conference method of reporting will probably find that it is particularly rewarding, even popular. They will find, also, that the teacher and the parent must prepare for their meeting. "Reporting," otherwise, may begin and end with an exchange of pleasantries, with almost nothing in between. In some communities, this is the time for the written report to be passed into the hands of the parent. Others have contended that this detracts from the conference, narrowing the scope of the conference and inhibiting the parent's contribution. This must be a local decision, of course.

Teachers of Flint, Michigan, are given the following suggestions for making oral reports to parents:[3]

1. Review the pupil's record and make definite plans before the interview.
2. Have a definite time for parent conference and the recording of appropriate data.
3. Have child's records and samples of work on hand to show the parent.
4. Schedule the conference in a setting of privacy and comfort.
5. Ask the parent to comment on the child's activities and interests.

---

[3] Flint Community Schools, *The Primary Cycle Reading Guide,* Flint, Michigan: Division of Instructional Services, Flint Public Schools, 1961, p. 8.

6. Be objective in attitude toward the child in expressing his strengths and weaknesses.
7. Ask the parent for suggestions and offer some alternatives if they are advisable.
8. Give constructive suggestions to help in the child's development.
9. Make sure that each parent leaves the conference with a positive attitude about his child's needs and his development.

If the conference is to be formalized, held at regularly-scheduled times each year, involving all parents, then it is probable that extra time will have to be provided for the teacher during the conference periods. This may be done by instituting a shortened day. By cutting the teaching day in half, the classroom teacher may comfortably plan for some five or six conferences. Thus, in five such days all parents may be met. As a concession to those few parents unable to come during daytime hours, one evening could also be set aside. Experience tells us that the efforts expended produce desirable results.

SUMMARY

No school district should contemplate a program of major change without first undergoing a period of intensive self-evaluation. The results of such a survey will point out most vividly what preliminary steps are needed to insure success.

These are the main areas that should be subjected to study:

1. The philosophy of the district
2. The district's expressed goals
3. Attitudes
    a. Of teaching staff
    b. Of building administration
    c. Of community

4. The existing curriculum
5. The system of reporting

Following the self-survey, a district can more intelligently plan and carry out a program of self-improvement.

7

Action for Change

In the previous chapter, I strongly recommended that a period of intensive self-evaluation precede any formal action toward change. The extent and the direction of change must stem from those findings. Assuming that there is no ultimate district, that is, a district where improvement is not required, we may focus on the *means* for effecting change. It is the purpose of this book to share certain successful practices that have led districts from the rigid practices of the mostly-graded school to the advantages of the more flexible ungraded kind of education. It has been my intention to interpret the ungraded school in its broadest sense: as a philosophy that touches upon every phase of a school or district program. Those who would develop only a program of continuous progress in reading have severely limited their goals. Simply removing grade labels is a kind of token gesture that invites the sneers of the ever-ready critics. Interage grouping must have a real purpose; it is not an end in itself. The totally ungraded school is all of these and more. To achieve the sophisticated goals of the ungraded school as well as the more obvious ones, each aspect of school program must work in harmony with all other aspects, and all aspects must find agreement with the guiding philosophy.

THE DEVELOPMENT OF PROFESSIONAL OBJECTIVES

Central School District No. 4 can be considered a classic example of a school district that subjected itself to intense self-analysis, and which then proceeded to remedial action. It attacked its problems on all fronts, using all of the resources at its command. Teams of teachers, administrators, and, to a lesser extent, lay members of the community participated in the all-out effort.

Following the study which lay bare the system's educational needs and shortcomings, a listing was made at the beginning of each year thereafter of the most desirable professional objectives for the district. Through the office of the superintendent, the objectives were published. Each of the objectives was assigned, some of them to teams of teachers representing different schools, some to teachers of each building, some to administrators on the building level, some to certain interested lay citizens. Certain objectives were assigned to central administrators. There were combinations of all of these groupings. There was overlapping of assignments. In all instances, each committee's role was to study the problems implied by the assigned objective, to describe practices in operation which supported the objective, and to recommend additional practices which would bring about greater improvement.

To point out the comprehensive nature of the professional objectives actually established during CSD 4's period of *action for change*, the entire listing for one year is shown. Some of it pertains directly to the instructional program. Other parts, while less directly affecting curriculum, are related, however remotely, to the educational process.

CENTRAL SCHOOL DISTRICT NO. 4
PROFESSIONAL OBJECTIVES

Introduction:

In the last several years Professional Objectives have been established as a guide for professional activities during the year. A number of staff members have participated in previous studies carried out and many worthwhile recommendations have been developed. Professional activity relating to Professional Objectives has laid the groundwork and pointed direction for improvement of professional service in many areas. However, a big task still remains in seeing that procedures and practices are being implemented throughout the entire district. A number of the Objectives for the coming year deal with implementation of, and continuation of, studies previously made.

Objectives listed below were developed by the Superintendent of Schools after consultation and contact with members of the professional staff, Board of Education, and certain community leaders interested in education.

Periodic reports of progress will be made during the coming school year at education meetings of the Board of Education. At the end of the school year, an evaluation meeting will be held at which time a frank appraisal will be made on progress in various Objectives.

OBJECTIVE 1   To improve and implement the program of professional staff supervision.

a. Refinement of teacher supervision program, including establishment of standardized orientation procedures and establishment of standards for observations, conferences, and staff evaluation.

b. Implementation of teacher supervision program throughout district preceded by intensive training of administrative and supervisory staff.

c. Refinement of evaluation criteria of administrators and supervisors based on quality of educational leadership.

OBJECTIVE 2   To conduct professional studies of teaching techniques and curriculum.

a. Establishment of statement of educational philosophy, including purposes and goals of school system.

b. Organization of existing curriculum materials on a vertical K through 12 basis and analysis to determine gaps and overlap in curriculum structure.

c. Establishment of system-wide curriculum committees in areas of greatest need.

d. Continued study of reading curriculum in grades K through 12.

e. Continued emphasis on provision for individual differences, including experimentation with team teaching and team learning.

f. Analysis of desirability of extending use of teaching machines.

g. Continued study of length of school day.

h. Continued study of philosophy and curriculum for junior high school.

i. Analysis and further development of present junior high school curriculum including articulation with junior high school.

OBJECTIVE 3   *To define responsibilities and relations of staff members.*

a. Complete development of job descriptions for all professional positions.

b. Complete development of job descriptions for all non-teaching positions.

c. Survey by County Civil Service to determine how present non-teaching positions compare with civil service classifications.

d. Continued analysis of effective utilization of staff, including teaching load, teaching schedules, etc.

e. Establishment of comprehensive program of professional advancement including broadened concept of in-service training provisions.

f. Analysis of present policy on extra remuneration for extra responsibilities and extent to which this should apply to any one individual.

OBJECTIVE 4   *To develop greater support and understanding of school programs.*

a. Continued development of school-community relations program.

b. Establishment of close working relationship with PTA's, seeking support for school budget, building referendum and state aid legislation.

c. Continued utilization of citizens committees for study of various special matters.

d. Development of educational film or films which can be shown to community groups illustrating school activities.

e. Utilization of "human resource" file.

OBJECTIVE 5 To initiate certain special school programs.
a. Establishment of basis for evaluating school programs, including possible use of outside accrediting or evaluative groups.
b. Analysis of cumulative record system, revising as needed.
c. Establishment of clear statement of policy regarding research and experimentation.
d. Continued study of district policy on homework and further development of information on study skills and study habits.
e. Study of the advisability of establishing a class for the emotionally disturbed.

OBJECTIVE 6 To effectively and economically operate school district.
a. Continued development of budget on year-round basis, with increased citizen participation.
b. Continued support for state aid legislation for education.
c. Continued implementation of procedures for system-wide inventory.
d. Analysis of business operations of the district.
e. Analysis of buildings and grounds operations.
f. Investigation of desirability of central storage for certain materials.

OBJECTIVE 7 To secure and retain a competent staff.
a. Continuation and refinement of year-round program of teacher recruitment.
b. Establishment of teacher salary schedule designed to minimize annual negotiating procedures.
c. Analysis of non-teaching salary schedules.
d. Analyse desirability of hiring permanent substitutes to be available to fill in new positions created or positions vacated.
e. Continued opportunities for the teacher organization to raise the professional stature of staff.

OBJECTIVE 8 To plan for new construction and use of present buildings to insure full-time sessions.
a. Development of educational specifications for new secondary school housing.
b. Analysis of rezoning required for best utilization of existing buildings.

OBJECTIVE 9   *To develop standardized Administrative Code and to recommend certain policy matters for inclusion in written school board by-laws.*

a. Refinement and standardization of preliminary Administrative Code.
b. Continued identification of certain areas needing policy decision by the Board of Education and developing recommendations accordingly.
c. Assisting the Board of Education in development of written Board by-laws.

OBJECTIVE 10   *To assist the School Board in attaining their objectives.*

a. Making recommendations and professional contacts with Board members through proper ethical channels.
b. Carrying out Board policies once adopted.

The *Professional Objectives* as listed have the earmarks of a full-blown educational crusade, and indeed it was. Its effectiveness hinged primarily upon keen leadership and upon follow-through. (Only a very few of the listed objectives will be referred to here.)

Through careful appointment of committee leaders, in the kind of direction given, the quality of response was controlled. Even then, tens of thousands of words had to be screened so that a reasonably coordinated year-end report could be made. To foster community interest, and to maintain staff enthusiasm and acceptance of the prodigious task, opportunities were provided for public presentations. The immense scope of the undertaking made it necessary to spread the presentations over several meetings.

Beyond the rendering of a printed report, the study activity had important side effects:

1. Professional staff were given opportunities for real participation in district improvement activities, and for self-improvement.
2. Professional staff, working together, developed a greater district unity.

3. Opportunities were given for recognition of individual professional competencies and leadership.
4. Through lay participation, a core of citizen supporters for change was brought into existence.

It is important, at this point, to relate the activities described to the notion of the ungraded school. As soon as a school district begins devoting its energies to providing service in fullest possible measure to the existing real children within its system, when it begins to express concern for the slower-learner and for the rapid learner, when it begins to reject the notion of school curriculum geared to that nonesuch, the average, then it is on the path toward the modern school—which we call the ungraded school.

Real leadership from the top is the crucial factor throughout the period of "the agonizing reappraisal" and during the planning-for-change phase. The superintendent who forcefully expresses his convictions on behalf of the individual pupil will find himself inducing the support needed for a successful period of transition. On the other hand, the lack of positive leadership might merely provoke a whirlwind of helter-skelter activity leading to an embarrassing and bewildering nowhere.

THE NEW PRODUCTS

The school district that consciously sets out to meet an expressed list of objectives may create for itself some important new products, or at least some handsomely altered older ones. Philosophy and goals, after being verbalized, do much to set the educational tone. The monumental job, of course, is the revision of curriculum in order to accommodate the concept of continuous progress. It is not essential, probably not possible, to complete such a large undertaking within a single year. It is enough initially that the job is undertaken. Acceptance and approval of the task may be considered a major gain.

Revising Curriculum

The revised curriculum must exceed the mere listing of topics to be covered. It must consider skills to be developed, cite sources of information for teacher as well as for student; it must recognize the need for sequential development. It ought to direct teachers to the means of satisfying the needs of the brighter student, of the slower student, *of each student.*

Who develops the curriculum? Local staff committees, to be sure. Certainly they may use models developed elsewhere, but they ought to be altered for specific local use.

Too large a committee is unwieldy, slow-moving, and frustrating. Yet, the smaller, more effective committee may be charged with not being truly representative. This latter problem is best overcome by having the committee composed of representatives of each building. These individuals are in a good position to make regular reports of progress to the staff members of their respective schools, getting general reaction, and bringing those reactions back to committee. Again, the quality of committee leadership will most determine the effectiveness of the committee.

Although continuous interaction with the staff as a whole tends to slow down the quantity of production, it serves to develop and maintain staff interest in the project. The project that is denied staff support may suffer critically.

Robert F. Savitt, superintendent of schools of Central School District No. 4 during its period of growth and educational change, developed an extensive report dealing with curriculum development in the district.[1] Following are selected excerpts which describe the process:

> . . . the following (are) convictions relative to curriculum change, and the vertical curriculum approach:

---

[1] Robert F. Savitt, *Development and Implementation of a Vertical Language Arts Curriculum.* (Mimeo) 1962.

A. Significant curriculum change can take place in a relatively short period of time.
B. A vertical curriculum in the field of language arts (and other curriculum areas also) can enhance educational opportunities for pupils.
C. An extensive amount of in-service education for staff members is required if a vertical curriculum is to be properly implemented.
D. The proper implementation of a vertical curriculum requires a re-analysis of organizational structure, deployment of staff and pupils, and a refinement of teaching materials.

. . . Concurrent with the establishment of district-wide educational objectives was the development of an administrative policy relating to democratic participation of staff in educational areas which stated in part:

"In order to attain a desirable educational environment and to expand educational opportunities for pupils, it is essential to draw upon the best professional thinking of teachers and administrators. Full utilization of the vast resources of our staff occurs when democratic procedures are in effect which encourage members of the professional staff to make suggestions regarding educational matters.

Past practice in this district has produced valuable results when staff members have been actively involved through proper channels in the study of various educational matters, such as curriculum, methodology, and other educational procedures and practices. A number of significant district-wide educational innovations have been aided by the system-wide participation of staff in the development of plans for these innovations. Forms of desirable staff participation include building and district-wide professional study committees and building faculty meetings where staff members can express themselves freely.

As a matter of administrative policy, central office administrators and building administrators are encouraged to provide a variety of opportunities for involvement of staff in the development of educational programs and procedures. Individual staff members are also encouraged to take advantage of opportunities provided for involvement in an analysis of educational matters. The administration, of course, ultimately reserves the right of final decision or recommendation after considering all available information."

. . . Early in their deliberations the staff committee became convinced that the curriculum being developed should be organized on a K through 12 vertical basis geared to provide instruction according to the varying needs of children. It was very soon evident to staff members involved that the modern reading program should not be restricted by artificial limits based on grade level achievement, but should, instead, be developed on the basis of levels of learning that children work through on the basis of their abilities. It also became evident . . . that any development of a vertical reading curriculum naturally leads to the inclusion of other areas in related language arts fields. Consequently, curricular materials were developed on a vertical basis in areas of literature including prose, poetry, and drama, and in the area of speaking and listening.

. . . a number of the teachers involved . . . started to break through grade level barriers in their individual schools so that when the vertical reading curriculum was completed, there were a number of living illustrations throughout the district indicating that a vertical language arts curriculum could provide valuable educational opportunities for pupils.

Based on the realization that a great amount of additional time was required in order to properly carry out curriculum innovations, the length of the teachers' day was expanded to provide for at least two hours of professional commitment a week above and beyond ordinary teaching responsibilities. Even this did not provide sufficient time for the detailed analysis involved in restructuring the language arts curriculum from a stilted grade-level concept to a flexible vertical curriculum with unlimited opportunities. Therefore, on several occasions during the school year certain members of the vertical curriculum committee were excused from their regular teaching responsibilities in order to spend full-day sessions developing or evaluating certain essential relevant materials.

The Board of Education, recognizing the potential value of the new curriculum approach, authorized expenditure of funds in the budget for summer employment of a number of committee members and for eight hours a day, five days a week, these people refined and finalized the vast amount of preliminary material developed by the entire committee.

IMPLEMENTATION OF THE CURRICULUM

Even though a number of staff members were involved in the development of the curriculum, a thorough program of in-service instruction was required before implementation of the curriculum could be effected. A series of meetings was established, conducted by members of the vertical language arts committee, including a general presentation to the Board of Education at a community-wide meeting attended by over 500 citizens. Workshops were held with district administrators on all levels concentrating on the role of the building administrator in implementing the vertical curriculum. A good portion of the orientation program for new and returning staff members at the beginning of the school year was devoted to a discussion of the vertical curriculum.

A series of building meetings was arranged wherein the building administrators and the building representatives on the system-wide curriculum committee had lengthy and detailed exchanges with the staff on the new approach. Additional district-wide assemblies were organized at which time the language arts specialists provided further insight into certain aspects and approaches of the vertical curriculum. These in-service training sessions were presented using closed-circuit television and several movies were made locally demonstrating teaching techniques inherent in the new teaching approach.

. . . It is not possible to modify curriculum in the manner described without having to face up to an evaluation of the effect that such curriculum changes inevitably have on organizational patterns . . . When a curriculum is based on the assumption that a child should be instructed according to his particular level and potential, the established patterns of grade organization become a constricting mold which prohibits the full value of the curriculum departure.

Modifying the Supervisory Program

Any program of supervision must be expected to work to reinforce the total educational program. This, too, must be expressed in writing. A document must exist which can be pointed to, referred to, which serves both teacher and supervisor as a guide and as a point of reference. The teacher must know that the purpose of supervision is to improve instruction, not to harass instructors . . . if this *is* the accepted notion.

Is formal classroom observation the sole means of supervision? How else might a supervisor help in bringing about the quality education being pursued? What are the specifics of the evaluation report?

A modern school must discard the check-the-height-of-the-window-shade kind of supervision. In its place there must be supervision which is sensitive to teacher strengths and needs, which provides help to individual teachers, to small groups of teachers, and to teachers as a whole group.

A formal program of teacher orientation to new mathematics may be required for the entire staff. Or, for one teacher, only an informal discussion on the ways to use filmstrips for motivation may be needed. In other instances, a teacher might best profit by witnessing a lesson in another classroom. The school's principal teacher will arrange for this.

One successfully employed supervisory technique is for the principal to observe a small group of teachers during a particular day or two, following this with an informal meeting of the observed teachers. Taking special care not to embarrass anyone, he may discuss some of the practices observed, ask others how they might have handled the same situations, exchange views on the real practices. Teachers are apt to be enthusiastic and keenly interested when they talk about themselves, their problems, and their points of view in dealing with the here and the now. Sharing is more likely to occur when the threat of criticism is removed.

There are, of course, many possible supervisory techniques, limited only by the imagination of the supervisor.

The ogre-administrator must become a remnant of the past. Potentially, the modern administrator is the main instrument for successfully inducing a quality school program. It is true that the competent teacher is best able to put into effect a good classroom program. Equally true is the fact that the competent administrator is needed to facilitate quality school-wide and district-wide programs.

IMPLEMENTATION OF NEW PROGRAMS

One of CSD 4's more significant district objectives was "the continued emphasis on provision for individual differences, including experimentation with team teaching and team learning."

This objective brought about the serious examination of methods of classroom instruction. In time it brought about gradual and important changes in classroom practice. Assuming that there had been much reading and discussion on team learning, it would hardly be expected that the decision would be made to initiate a team learning program in *each* of the schools and with *all* of the staff. Instead, only one or two members of the staff—those most interested and enthusiastic—would incorporate the plan. After a period of experimentation, they would report their experiences to other members of the faculty, formally and otherwise. Eventually, provided that experience proved the merits of the idea, staff members would be invited to observe the program. Gradually, other staff members would follow suit.

Other changes throughout the curriculum—e.g., the use of the multi-level speller, the introduction of certain programmed materials—would take place in the same manner. The program would begin in one or two classrooms; if found desirable, it would gradually be brought into each of the appropriate classrooms. The teachers would themselves evaluate and determine acceptance. The administrator's role would be to provide the necessary leadership.

The complexity of a new program determines the extensiveness of effort in effecting full implementation. A switch from the graded plan of reading to the plan of continuous progress requires the closest of attention to detail, the fullest understanding of all participating staff, and the most careful supervision.

Perhaps the ideal way of dealing with an elaborate new program is through in-service training. The individual or group of individuals providing the guiding force behind the newly-developed program might well be entrusted with the task of developing the details of the in-service course. It is not sufficient to put together a shiny new guide, trusting the power of the written word. Teachers need the opportunity to raise questions, to ask for more elaborate explanations on certain details; they need to feel that the new program is something of special value. A lifeless paper guide is no match in this respect for the enthusiastic in-service instructor able to give more information and helpful reassurance.

Nor can the building administration be denied full opportunity to keep abreast of new developments within their district. Unless they are included in a comprehensive in-service training program, they will lose their rights to their roles as instructional leaders. Supervision loses impact when the supervisor is less than knowledgeable about the subject or method he supervises.

The most effective in-service courses are those which deal most closely to the realities of the local situation. The course work which pertains to the theories of instruction is of greatest value in the university. It is a mistake to imitate the university in a setting which calls for a confrontation of the local situation as it really exists. The better tomorrow is best reached when those who would move in that direction tread solidly along the paths of today's reality.

SUMMARY

Action for change may begin after a district takes the opportunity to analyze its strengths, weaknesses, needs, and inclinations. After establishing district objectives based on local considerations, professional leadership designs a format aimed at attacking the objectives. Working committees, composed in a variety of ways, are assigned the tasks outlined in the published goals. The results of the study activity are ultimately published; reports may be given orally, also, in the form of public presentations.

Certain changes take place in the school program as a result.

In most instances, these start gradually. With experience, the decision is made to expand or eliminate the new practices. In time, many new district practices come into being.

Change in practices in the classroom may well call for change in supervisory procedure. The supervisory program would be expected to work in support of the developing programs and within the framework of the pronounced philosophy.

During any transitional period the success of the transition will depend heavily upon the quality of leadership that is exercised. A plan of implementation is required. Depending upon the complexity of program, new programs may be put into effect through providing opportunity for discussion, explanation, and observation for certain periods of time. For the major change, a thoroughly planned in-service course is recommended. In-service education is as important—or more important—for administrators as it is for the classroom teacher.

8

Community Support: An
Essential
Consideration

Parents have become a formidable force in modern public education. A school or school district that wishes to inaugurate a major new program has to face the task of gaining community support and approval. This is particularly true with the ungraded school. An important aspect of the program is parental understanding of the program's main goals, accompanied by parental cooperation.

In the pioneer communities, the problem of implementation listed most frequently was that of community understanding and acceptance.[1] Another problem high on the list was the matter of orienting parents coming into the community. Following is a sampling of comments related to community relations:

---

[1] Reference is made here to the author's doctoral study wherein a questionnaire was developed and submitted to some 44 communities that had been identified as the earliest of the ungraded schools. Thirty-six of these gave response. See Appendix A.

1. Ungrading the entire school worked well but perhaps ungrading one year at a time might have been better. The number of parent contacts required was enormous and time-consuming. In moving one year at a time these contacts would have been reduced quite substantially.
2. Parental understanding is difficult to achieve. Many parent conferences were necessary.
3. Our public relations was less than satisfactory. We might have planned more thoroughly.
4. Parent orientation was not good.
5. Even after our experience we are not sure how fully parents should be involved.
6. We did not have enough public involvement; therefore, we had some difficulties gaining support.

Nor are the newer members of the fast-growing "ungraded school club" able to ignore the need to devise means of gaining parental approbation. Personal, informal contacts with other principals of ungraded schools have established this strongly held opinion: Only the foolhardy school would invite public protest through *not* developing a program of public relations designed to "sell" the new educational product. Moreover, the selling cannot be incidental, casual, or poorly conceived. It must compare favorably, if only in terms of planning and effort, with the pitch and patter of the Madison Avenue gang. Happily, the schools have one special advantage—the sincerity of motive.

PARENTAL INVOLVEMENT

It has been mentioned previously that parents might well be invited to join, as lay participants, in the development of district philosophy and goals. Moreover, as a district progresses in its quest for improvement, from self-analysis to study, to introduction of certain smaller programs in limited numbers of classes, it is especially desirable to take available opportunities for reports of progress to the community. When these reports stem, also, from *key community figures,* who have had either limited assignment, or special orientation, the impact upon community is more likely to be positive in nature. The "key figures" may be active and respected PTAers or others in the limelight of civic matters who have demonstrated interest and understanding of public education's needs.

Public support must be solicited in the earliest stages of the struggle for improvement, not just prior to the initiation of bold new programs. Lay participation, also, begins at the beginning.

There is a danger that is obvious to school people, one that makes them uncomfortable with the idea of parent involvement. The untrained but vocal citizen may desire and even find opportunity to make decisions regarding instructional program . . . unless this possibility is anticipated and provisions are made to prohibit this. It is simple enough to establish ground rules for lay participation prior to the first act of active involvement. They may be advised that their involvement may be in study, in presenting reports, and in hearing the reports of others, with the understanding that decision-making must remain in the hands of the professionals. The knowing beforehand is what will save the finger-pointing, the desk-thumping, and the estrangement of needed friends.

THE MONTHLY DISTRICT NEWSLETTER

It is a fairly common practice for school districts to send reports from time to time to the home of the taxpayer. Those school-to-home communications can be especially valuable, but frequently a school district lessens the potential good of the medium through certain unnecessary failures. These suggestions are made:

1. Develop an attractive and standard format, using offset printing as opposed to mimeo, if possible cost-wise.
2. Establish a regular deadline. Adhere to it. Let it be known that the newsletter will be sent home every month at the same time.

3. Mail the newsletter home, rather than entrust it to small and busy hands. The extra cost is worth it. However, be certain that the mailing-list is up-to-date.

4. If the services of a professional or near-professional writer are not available in the district, it might be well to at least solicit some advice on style. The drearily-written piece makes little impact. The over-bubbly "we-are-the-greatest" amateur pieces are offensive. While the newsletter may be needed to deal with non-instructional areas, it should be the policy of the editor to include reports of significance regarding instruction in each issue. It must be emphasized: these should be written as factual reports, not as immodest bits of self-praise.

5. The occasional double-size issue is an effective means of showing emphasis. For example, all the space in such an issue may be used to feature a report on the introduction of a new program; or the extra space may be utilized during American Education Week; or for a special purpose as determined locally.

6. Just as our advertising brethren frequently employ the gradual lead-up to a new product, the school district that expects to develop important new products ought not to blurt out the news suddenly. In the manner of one of those endless radio or TV serials, continuing reports should be made of the progress of study teams, of small scale experiments, and such.

PRINCIPAL-TO-PARENT BULLETIN

For the principal who enjoys the opportunity to put some of his thinking on paper, an excellent means of building up public acceptance is through the use of a regular principal-to-parent bulletin. This need not be lengthy nor need the contents be geared for "the big sell." From the point of view of a parent, the communication that originates from the mystical land of central office is of less consequence than the communication that comes from the school where his child is entrusted for long hours daily. Moreover, the building principal is ordinarily recognized as the key figure in the building, the person who sets the educational tone and who ultimately is responsible for the goings-on within that building.

The bulletin might deal with a number of prosaic matters: parking in the bus loop, the problem of supplying the youngsters with sneakers, or the matter of regular attendance. But it must also cast the principal in the role of educational leader. The larger part of the bulletin would deal with matters of educational consequence: an interpretation of the significance of the new mathematics; the newest materials for individualization; the importance of the free-swinging kindergarten program, and such.

So as not to provoke annoyance, jargon ought to be screened out of such a bulletin. It can be done. Equally bad is the talking-down style. The bulletin should be kept lean and factual, tinged most delicately with available humor. Self praise remains offensive.

The time will come when parents must be informed, in a variety of ways, that the school which cares for their children is going to be ungraded. If the parents had previously been advised that the district was concerned with improvement, that various new practices were being initiated, that the ungraded school was being implemented in dozens of schools throughout the country . . . successfully, that the school was participating in a district-wide study of the potential advantages of such a program for the district, then the announcement does not hit with sudden and melodramatic force. When the announcement is made by the educational leader of the school who has been in regular communication with his community, the probability of community confidence in the idea is increased.

PARENT, PRINCIPAL, COFFEE, AND CONVERSATION

Sadly enough, and frequently enough, an upset parent will blurt out the fact that "when the other mothers and I were having coffee the other morning, we all agreed that the school does not ...." (principals may fill in the blanks.)

The coffee klatch is a time for good fellowship, but it is also a time that is used fruitfully by those who would sow seeds of discontent for whatever dark and sinister motives they may have (such as revenge for not getting a bus pass . . . or because little Susan is not in the top reading group.) The principal is not entirely helpless in this. He may indeed counterattack!

If the workload permits, and if public relations has not already gotten out of hand, and if the principal likes coffee, he may extend an open invitation for parents to meet with him over coffee some Tuesday morning (or whatever day or time is most convenient). At that time he may have an open agenda, discussing those things which appear to be of special interest and concern to the parents attending.

Publicity for this kind of informal meeting should be handled by the PTA. This is an obvious help to the principal, but, perhaps more importantly, the PTA is not by-passed or slighted. A foolish situation would be a public relations gain through the additional effort, negated by a jilted and therefore antagonistic PTA. It could happen.

THE PARENT-TEACHER ORGANIZATION

If you know of a school where attendance at PTA meetings reflects a kind of apathy on the part of parents, you know of a school which is very much like all schools. This being true, how much attention should an administrator devote to the organization? Is that attention wasted?

The PTA is a sleeping giant, even the local units. It can be destructive for it is not really controlled too well by the well-intentioned state and national leaders. School officials would do well to encourage the "good guys" of the community to lend their talents to the organization. The "bad guys" serve as a nucleus for malcontents and the semi-professional troublemakers. They take over when school officials *tolerate* "the pesky organization." A building principal who focuses his attention on his parent-teacher organization can influence the shape of that organization. Certainly he has the support of his staff and all the votes therein. (Doesn't he?)

After a building principal makes his thinking known, it is likely that his executive board, in his presence, will adopt his stance (or a reasonable facsimile thereof) on each issue that presents itself. What is important is that the building principal is present and does make his position known at the executive sessions. Otherwise, the cartoon that shows the one housewife talking to another suggesting, "Want to shoot your mouth off? Let's go to the PTA meeting" becomes less than humorous, much too factual.

As a sleeping giant, PTA has its greatest potential during periods of crisis. The organization is there for communicating to the community at large. A PTA that is honestly for the schools and for quality education has the ability to reach out to a large portion of the community, to give it correct information. The method of presentation, the personal touch, is especially effective.

The building principal that keeps key segments of his PTA informed on the developing instructional program of his school will probably find disciples in the key people. Introduction to the concept of the ungraded school should be gradual. The exploration must be thorough. It is not a one-session topic. There should be involvement. The group that gets an opportunity to participate, as through study, and reporting on that study, will feel closer ties to the idea.

THE VITAL PERIOD

The activities during the time period just prior to the actual initiation of the ungraded school and immediately after the program has begun is of vital importance in terms of public cooperation.

Poorly thought out, these activities may bring on headaches that will detract from the joy of bringing forth the fine new program.

The large group meeting

It will be necessary to call together those parents whose children will be directly affected by the change. If the decision is made to drop grade labels for grades 1 and 2, then the parents of the kindergarteners and the first graders should receive the invitation to attend the meeting. To invite others is to enlarge the changes of harassment.

Even before the meeting begins, certain preparatory arrangements should have been made. The teachers to be involved should be present, as well as well-informed key lay citizens. If an experienced expert is available for a part of the presentation, *he may be of real benefit provided that his interpretation is not in conflict with yours.* This, too, has happened.

Bear in mind that one of the main reasons for education and other social sciences being "behind the times" is resistance to change. The ungraded school must not be hailed as a radical departure threatening the security of the children and the community at large. Instead, it is another step in the direction of highest quality education. The following is page 4 of a 4-page brochure developed by myself for the parents of Parkway School. It stresses the points just made. It was distributed at the large group meeting.

FINALLY

THIS IS NOT, IN FACT, A NEW AND DARING, AND ULTRA-DIFFERENT PROGRAM FOR PLAINVIEW. WE HAVE LONG AGO ADOPTED THE GOALS AND PHILOSOPHY OF THE NONGRADED SCHOOL. YEAR BY YEAR WE HAVE DEVELOPED TECHNIQUES AND HAVE USED MATERIALS WHICH PROMOTE INDIVIDUALIZATION OF INSTRUCTION. AS STATED BEFORE, WE ARE SIMPLY AND EASILY TAKING ANOTHER STEP IN THE DIRECTION OF OUR GOALS.

As was true before ungrading, we are going to report honestly and factually the academic progress of your children . . . we are going to maintain comprehensive records . . . we are going to teach the 3 R's plus . . . but we are hoping to do all of these things better, more efficiently, and in acknowledgment of our understanding of child growth and development.

STEPS TO HIGHEST QUALITY

7. Organization for Individualization

6. Techniques of Individualization

5. Materials of Individualization

4. Quality Staff

3. Curriculum

2. Goals

1. Philosophy

In the major part of the presentation, it must be pointed out emphatically that the school is already ungraded to a degree (teachers make provision for individual differences, materials in use are geared to the child, perhaps your reading program already concedes to the notion of continuous progress.) It may be indicated that most studies outrightly claim, or suggest, these advantages:

1. There is an increase in pupil achievement in reading and in other academic areas.
2. The problems relative to retention and acceleration are eliminated or lessened.
3. Greater flexibility in pupil placement permits the most appropriate pupil placement.
4. The de-emphasizing of the artificial grade concept lessens pressures on pupils and teachers.
5. The less wholesome kinds of pupil competition are reduced.
6. The concessions to the realities of child growth and development improves teacher morale, fosters greater enthusiasm, facilitates instruction; hence, it produces better instructional practices.

Following the presentation, it is usual to have a question-and-answer period. At this time, the building principal may give teachers or others who have knowledge of the program opportunities to respond. This may suffice. In the event that the tone of the questions takes on a consistent negative quality, a single question from the principal may dramatically change the meeting atmosphere:

"Are there members of the audience who are able to make positive statements about the school program as it exists and who, on that basis, are able to trust our motives as well as our ability to provide a good educational program for their children?"

To be sure, posing such a question is a risk. What a let-down it would be to get no reaction! However, it is more likely you may know your audience and may even be able to ask this of particular individuals. Cynics and dissenters have been overwhelmed by clear and strong statements of support. The listeners, those who choose only to absorb or to silently react to the expressions, are influenced by the degree of support evidenced.

For the benefit of those parents who were unable or unwilling to attend the large group meeting, a brochure ought to be available. These brochures should contain the key statements made in the large group presentation, without being laboriously detailed. They may be distributed at the meeting, and a large supply held for those who will later make inquiry. "New" parents, those coming into the district, should receive copies at the time of registering their children.

In Edmonds, Washington, the PTA of the Maple Park School distributed ballots following the large group presentations. Parents voted as to whether or not they were in agreement with the proposal to ungrade the primary section of the school. Results were as follows:

1st Grade	130 possible ballots	96 returned	81 yes	13 no
2nd Grade	105 possible ballots	70 returned	56 yes	14 no

3rd Grade	137 possible ballots	113 returned	97 yes	18 no
Totals	372 possible	279 returned	234 yes	45 no

The democratic approach was obviously successful in this instance. A follow-up questionnaire was developed after the program had been in operation for a time. This, too, showed the degree of public support. (For specific results, see Appendix E.)

One-to-one conferences

After the program is in operation, the building principal will find it necessary to cope with almost random questions from parents concerned with various aspects of the program, primarily from those parents whose children are in the inter-age classes. These are excellent opportunities to eliminate potential small pockets of resistance. The principal is wise to set up one-to-one conferences. At these conferences, he can point out that the children, in these classes particularly, are given some real advantages. The best qualified teachers have been selected for these classes, and whatever the educational instruments used, it is true that the classroom teacher is, by far, the most important factor in instruction. Further, these classes usually have the smallest enrollment, thereby making it easier for the teacher to give each child a larger share of attention. All other statements must stem from the expressed concerns of the parent.

In the one-to-one conference, parents are ordinarily appreciative of the courteous attention they receive from the building principal. They respond well. Chances are good that the largest number of them will become proponents of the program.

The one-to-one conference is superior to additional large group meetings in that the anxieties of some will not be imposed on large numbers of other parents.

When to stop

After the initial excitement dies down, after the parent inquiries have been satisfied, it is time to behave as though the program in operation is a rather ordinary matter. Parents should be informed as to programs within the ungraded program, e.g., the operation of the new math within the primary unit, or the multi-level spelling program in the intermediate section, or the significance of kindergarten readiness, etc. To harp away at the philosophy of ungradedness after the difficult transitional phase is to invite greater parental involvement than is necessary. The best salesmen know when the product is sold; they do not endanger their sale by bullish overselling.

The second year of the ungraded school should run more smoothly than the first. Five years later, assuming the program is a good one, it should be accepted with the naturalness that typified the reaction of parents to the graded school.

Finally

In this chapter, a variety of suggestions have been made relative to inducing community support of the ungraded philosophy and program. Undoubtedly, there are many other public relations procedures that would be helpful. These must be determined according to the talents of the professional staff, including administration—if not especially administration—and according to the kind of community that is being served. Going overboard in seeking public favor is as foolish as pretending that public support is unnecessary. While support is needed, the main task of the professional force is to provide a program of quality instruction. A certain degree of time spent in providing the public with information is a worthy investment; when it goes to extremes, we are using time better spent in program development.

SUMMARY

The school that hopes to successfully inaugurate a modern new educational program, one that wrenches the school from tradition, must cope with the need for public support. The experience of communities that have made the change underlines this need.

Parental involvement, written communication, formal and informal meetings between school and public are strongly suggested. The potential of the parent-teacher organization ought to be realized, and used.

The time period immediately preceding the official inauguration of the program until some months after the program is in operation is identified as the vital period; however, public relations on behalf of the program should begin long before.

There is a danger in over-selling, as there is a danger in investing excessive time and energy in public relations at the expense of program. The kind of public relations, its extent, depends upon the special talents of staff and the characteristics of the community being served.

9

The Role of the Building Principal

In the elementary school of not so long ago, the building principal may have been appointed to his position because he was the lone male on the staff, perhaps the physical education instructor. Or he may never have had contact with the elementary school, but, as the reasoning went, the principalship paid a more liveable salary and should go to a man with a family to support. Why not? Was it not the principal's function to scold children, to check attendance registers, and to conduct fire drills? What else was there, except maybe to check the height of the green window-shades? How much training is required for that kind of responsibility?

It is not my intent to belittle physical education instructors . . . or males. Rather, I wish to express my delight in the fact that the role of the elementary principal generally has been upgraded. The modern community, particularly one that is aware of the immense potential of elementary education, is not going to tolerate the poorly managed or the unmanaged elementary school. No community should.

Goodbye to the illogical elementary school stereotypes of not so long ago: a school staffed with sour-faced spinsters training unsmiling kids their letters and their numbers (the three R's), with the highlight of the week being the spelling bee. Undoubtedly, the image has not been cast out entirely, but it has faded considerably. You will find a relationship between modern program and modern principal.

The major share of responsibility for the successful inauguration of the ungraded school rests with the building principal. Without his overall support, his guidance, his supervision, the chances for an effective execution of program are lessened dramatically. No superintendent or assistant superintendent in charge of instruction is going to circumvent this key administrator in putting the program into operation. The offices of central administration function best when they act as helpers to the building principal. The enlightened central office administrator knows full well that the building administrator, daily in direct contact with his staff, his community, his youngsters, is in the best possible position for understanding his building needs and for providing the kind of daily leadership that is required in program development.

Actually, it is usually a building principal who promotes the initial move toward ungrading, for he sees best the conflict between modern program and gradedness. The central office administrator then becomes either the facilitator or the impediment.

The role of the modern elementary principal is a complex one. As the instructional leader about to guide his professional staff along the path of innovation, the role becomes especially demanding. All skills are called into play. Weaknesses that otherwise might be kept in shadow are magnified.

PRIOR TO THE FORMAL INTRODUCTION
OF THE UNGRADED PROGRAM

Once having determined that a school will move into the ungraded program, the principal of that school must assume the myriad tasks that are a part of laying the essential groundwork. These tasks may not ordinarily be set according to any easily established sequence. They are only specified after the over-all needs of the school are uncovered. Frequently, the activities are carried on concurrent with each other.

Preparing the Staff

Ultimately, it is the teaching staff that succeeds or fails in putting a program into effect. When the classroom teacher withholds support, openly or otherwise, that program is damned!

The finest professional relationship that can be developed between teacher and supervisor is one where there can be honest exchange of expression. Where this exists, the building principal can estimate with relative ease the scope of the work needed with the staff. Unfortunately, there are many situations where the staff assumes the pose of mutes, listening, silently, apparently absorbing the principal's monologue . . . but possibly not. Worse, a staff may "yes" its boss at every opportunity, for experience may have shown them that this is what he wants. When either of these latter situations prevails, the danger to *any* program is great.

The details of staff preparation are many. They must be kept in mind by the principal as he goes about each of his supervisory tasks. In all of his contacts with staff, formal and informal, large group meeting, small group meeting, or one-to-one meeting, he must hammer away at the idea that the primary function of the school is to serve each and every student, to design programs to fit each student. This is the adopted philosophy of the district and this is what the school is committed to implement.

The following are some of the items that may well be taken up at full faculty meetings, items that serve to develop the tone for the approaching birth (of the ungraded program):

1. Research findings relative to retention and acceleration
2. The value of readiness activities in kindergarten
3. The meaning of "continuous progress" in relation to reading
4. The advantages of programmed materials
5. Recent research on how children learn
6. Techniques for instructional individualization

These are only a sampling of the possible topics for discussion relative to the ideas inherent in any ungraded plan. No full faculty meeting should ever be allowed to deal exclusively with "junk" items, that is, items that deal with the possibly essential but unstimulating administrative trivia—problems of behavior in the cafeteria, changes in schedule for instrumental music, and such. When trivia is the sole or the primary focus of the building principal, it is not surprising to discover that the staff of the school is reluctant to pursue educational innovation. Intuitively, or outrightly, they know that leadership is vital to success. The hack principal is no inspiration.

In the one-to-one conference, where the principal and teacher discuss a lesson observed, what is the principal concern? Does he find it necessary to belabor the mechanics of the lesson—the use of the chalkboard, the arrangement of furniture, the quality of the teacher's voice, the manner in which children hold their writing instruments, and such? These contribute, beyond a doubt, but these cannot be the emphasized segments of the lesson. The principal must demonstrate his greatest concern for the children. Was this work repetitious, unnecessary for a particular group? Was it not beyond certain others? Wouldn't it be proper to commend the teacher for catering to the different abilities, if this were true?

Perhaps the principal knows of available materials that would benefit the follow-up lessons, in terms of individual children. If certain teacher weaknesses are noted, what can the principal do, beyond the evaluation, to provide assistance? How about a demonstration lesson, perhaps by the principal, which would most easily impress the teacher with the possible other ways of handling the subject?

The principal doesn't always have to chair each meeting that takes place within the school. He ought to be able to entrust members of the professional staff with leading group discussion. Certainly the psychologist, an expert on inner motivation as it pertains to learning, a scholar on the topic of the individual, ought to be able to play a major role in redirecting attention to the individual. One teacher ought to be able to report on his progress with the programmed material that only his class has.

For the principal there are endless teaching opportunities whereat the new emphasis gets additional airings. He has to be alert to them, using them, endlessly promoting, promoting, promoting the case for ungradedness. Over-using the terminology can be a bore for staff. The special new words ought to be used with studied restraint. Interest must be in the action, not the vocabulary.

In the selection of materials for the program, it is the responsibility of the principal to participate in the examination of new materials, and to insure that the items selected will contribute to the most effective implementation of the overall program. In some cases, it might be best to put the more radically new material in only a few classes. All decisions relative to new material must be made after weighing the ability of staff to incorporate many new materials. However, it is difficult to ask teachers to feature individualization unless they are given the wherewithal for effecting this style of program.

Selection of material cannot be done in isolation by the building principal, if only because of staff resentment of such procedure.

They will be required to carry out the program. As practitioners of the teaching art, their judgments are especially valuable, particularly if they fall within the framework of district philosophy.

After it is seen that the staff has accepted the newly-espoused philosophy, after they have begun to develop some of the required techniques and have put them to use in the classroom together with the most appropriate of materials, it is time to talk to the staff about the significance of a formal adoption of the program. Among the vital issues to be thrashed out, to reach accord on, are the following:

1. The significance of the new grouping plan and the role to be played by each member of the professional team in the grouping procedure.
2. The development of a unified vocabulary relating to the program, and the need to conscientiously utilize it in all references to program. (The tendency remains to talk about Grade 1 and 2, etc., about grade level, and the like. The point is stressed because of some obvious embarrassment that could develop, particularly in dealing with the public.)
3. The need for teachers to treat all instruction, to the extent possible, in terms of the concept of continuous progress, to seek self-improvement in terms of techniques of individualization.
4. The need to inform, or educate, parents regarding the goals of the program, particularly as they relate to their children.

Only those teachers who are to be directly involved in the official ungrading need to work intensively in preparation. Others may be invited as observers from time to time, perhaps representatives of the remaining grade levels. In all instances, it is especially desirable to keep minutes of the meetings that take place. Each teacher should keep a file, having all material dealing with the program in ready reference.

In noting "teachers who are to be directly involved," it can be seen that the various specialists, those who are to deal in any way with the ungraded classes, are to be directly involved. If the principal sees fit, their meetings may be held separately . . . but they ought not to be overlooked.

Preparing the Non-Instructional Personnel

Unless the non-instructional personnel of the building are given a period of orientation, there is a very good chance they will un-do some of the hard-earned progress that is made. The secretarial staff will undoubtedly need less orientation since they will be handling much of the paper work dealing with the program. However, this should not prevent some discussion on the roles they need to fill to assist in the implementation of the program. In interviewing new entrants, the secretary might well say:

"Our school is known as an ungraded school. Here is some literature that may clarify that for you. I am sure you will be pleased with the quality of the educational program here. Incidentally, if you'd like, our building principal will be happy to discuss our program in relation to your children."

Something much worse could happen, such as:

"I know they don't use grades any more, but I really don't quite understand what is happening. Maybe you'd better ask the principal."

The friendly custodian, who deals frequently enough with public and children, is not helpful when he constantly asks children: "What grade are you in?" or constantly refers to grade in his brief interactions with the public.

Of course there is no weighing the degree of discomfort or actual harm that is done by the little "slips." Since they can be avoided, they ought to be. Moreover, the inclusion of the non-instructional staff in educational matters fosters good employee relations, as well as good public relations.

The Principal and Central Office Administration

Unless the building principal keeps central administration informed (and this holds true graded or ungraded), it can happen that all of the other matters that cry for the attention of that harassed office will feast upon his fair share. The building principal cannot afford to deny his building the nourishments of that influential bee-hive, particularly if his building is treading the road to innovation. While the ungraded school does not call for vast new expenditures, there are demands that can justifiably be made. Specifically, the program must have a larger number of textbooks (for the multi-basal approach), and therefore more teacher editions. And if there are available programmed materials, which allow individualization, then the ungraded school ought to have them, also. If there is a policy on the experience-level of teachers (to save money the district might strongly encourage the hiring only of neophytes), this point might be also be stretched in order to get the best available person. The building principal must so advise central office of needs. Incidentally, if these things are not accomplished during the pre-innovation period, it is more difficult after the program is put into operation.

The active interest of central administration in the new educational program has a stimulating effect upon staff and community. Recognizing this, the principal might well involve the superintendent, or the assistant superintendent in charge of instruction, in some of the faculty meetings, or the public meetings. However, in those instances, the building principal must take the major role, while the central office administrator plays the part of supporting giant.

Who would deny that the central office administration does serve also in providing guidance? From that point ought to come a wealth of suggestions on dealing with problems as they arise. There are resources there and they ought to be tapped, as needed.

Preparing the Children

In the activity-filled period just prior to the official inauguration of the ungraded school, it is conceivable that the need to orient the children might be overlooked. . .a humorous possibility. It is surprising to see the degree to which some of the youngsters have learned to become grade-conscious.

Getting the children to appreciate the fundamental reasons for the forthcoming changes is a worthwhile endeavor. In effect, we are revising their sense of values relative to their personal school goals. In the minds of so many the greatest achievement was "graduating" from one grade into the next. The greatest worry was the possibility that this might not happen. If developed properly, the new emphasis, the new major goal would become: learning as best as one could while finding daily enjoyment in the learning process.

How do we accomplish this change in attitude? As with other subject matter, the teaching is done best when the teacher goes beyond the telling-them approach. Children, even the youngest of them, can treat this as a topic of everyday living. They can participate in discussion, asking questions, offering opinions, and reaching general conclusions. The skillful teacher gets the desirable result.

The principal's role in this goes beyond just advising the teaching staff that the children should receive orientation. With the staff he ought to plan the best kind of unified approach, with differences in presentation depending upon the maturity of the children. To give the changeover special status, it is an effective procedure to have an assembly period as a starting-off point at which time the principal introduces the idea, leaving it to the classroom teacher to follow through in the classroom.

Public relations-wise, the child who finds the idea something good will translate this feeling back home, where the anxious parents (and we know there are many of them) may be dramatically wringing their hands, muttering "What are they doing to my poor child?" The reassurances of the children may spare many a parent-principal confrontation.

Miscellany

Every effort should be made to anticipate all of the minor details that will have to be dealt with during that crucial first year. Does the report card accommodate the program? Have the various records been examined closely so that the necessary changes will be made in order to avoid conflict? How will attendance records take to the ungrading? Has a procedure been established for taking in new students during the course of the year. . . and for identification of "grade level" for those children leaving the school to go to a graded one?

DURING THE FIRST OFFICIAL YEAR OF OPERATION

After that year of intensive preparation, it must come to pass that the September of the first official year of the ungraded program will arrive. The extent and the quality of preparation will be reflected in the degree of smoothness of initial operation. If the public-relations aspect had received the right amount and kind of attention, then parental harassment will be minimal. Difficulties that present themselves will probably highlight those areas which needed a little more or a better kind of handling.

Crises, small and large, often present challenge to the building principal. For some of us, it is a way of life. Perhaps we may be likened to firemen, having the responsibility to react to the flames (of crises) as soon as we are aware of their existence. That, incidentally, makes the difference between an effective or an ineffective fireman: the ability to smother flames before they do extensive damage. The building principal who mimics the short-sighted isolationist, ever surrounding himself with the walls of his office, away from the action, will eventually find that the isolation has worked to the detriment of his school and himself.

For Information-gathering: The Informal Tour

Perhaps a panicky pace is somewhat melodramatic and unnecessary. Nevertheless, the building principal must secure strong and comfortable walking shoes and constantly explore the various physical areas comprising the building that is his overall responsibility. Periodic, frequent tours may turn up information that can be acted on for a better school operation.

Examine a few examples:

A stroll down the corridor of the primary section will reveal that teachers generally are working with groups of children, or with the class as a whole. Teachers will be at their desks, or moving about, or in the reading corner. Children will be sitting and listening, or they will be actively participating, or they will be engaged in a variety of activities. A general school tone will be revealed: warm teacher-pupil relationships, or tenseness, or teacher-dominance. Since one-frame-doesn't-make-a-game, the impressions received must be reinforced or altered by a number of additional strolls.

In the early morning, when some parents are escorting their youngsters to school, when other parents are having quick conferences with some staff members, or even when parents meet in hallways for neighborly discussion, there is an opportunity for the principal to assess general parental attitude, their response to the school as they know it. Nor is it unusual for some parent-principal small talk to take place during these hallway encounters, These have some value.

After the school has been in session for a period of time, a look about the storeroom or storerooms may serve a purpose. Are there materials or books in storage that might better be in the hands of the classroom teachers, that they might not know is in existence? Isn't the multi-text approach more easily effected when those texts are in the classroom?

The "tour" is potentially helpful to the building administrator at any time, but it is especially advantageous during the beginning stages of the new operation.

Principal-Staff Meetings

In the first year of the official ungrading, the number of staff meetings will probably increase substantially. The most effective kind of meeting, one that can deal most directly and most intensively with the subject for discussion, has smaller numbers of participants.

Specialists (the art teacher, music teacher, and others) and principal may talk more freely, with fuller participation, when the meeting group is limited to the specialists and the building principal. The focus is then justifiably on the problems and practices of those specialists.

As previously noted, a profitable administrative technique is a meeting involving the principal and those teachers who have been formally observed on a particular day. Whatever the lesson observed, the principal may relate what he has seen to a particular idea—as, perhaps, the matter of providing for individual children—and use the lesson solely as a jumping-off point, departing to such topics as: the planning of the lesson, the activities that preceeded the lesson, other ways of meeting the expressed goals of the lesson, etc. He may solicit ideas from any of the others observed. The principal must most definitely utilize the statesman's finesse in directing the exchanges that will take place. If teachers are humiliated, then the purpose of such a meeting has been perverted.

More than at any other time, the principal should be in and out of the classrooms, formally and informally, for long periods of time and for brief moments. Beyond observing, he must be prepared to offer positive suggestions, including utilization of materials which, if not in the classroom, he would make every effort to secure.

While the need for the greatest possible communication between teacher and principal is stressed, it must be done with the realization that the teacher is particularly sensitive to the many pressures that accompany the embarkation on a new program. While it should always be so, at this time especially the principal's role must be as an available and very helpful resource person. The spectre of the stiff, dead-pan evaluator could too easily unsettle and undermine the real efforts of the teacher.

As pointed out emphatically elsewhere, one of the best services that the building principal can provide is to see to it that the classroom teacher has a class make-up which comes very close to what was intended during the grouping procedures. When he sees that there are misplacements, he must exert the required effort to make corrections.

A Principal's Experience Log

To profit from successes and errors, the recording of the many experiences relating to the unfolding program is useful. This kind of experience log, viewed periodically, is an aid in evaluating the overall program. Later, in presenting a report of progress to other building administrators, the details of experience are usually more welcome than a listing of generalizations. Some of this material may well be developed by staff members: classroom teachers and specialists.

For the Interage Class: the Sociometric Test

Of all the features of the ungraded school, the one requiring the most justification in order to meet public *and* professional concern is the interage class. The bugaboo producing the greatest anxiety is the social differences between the mingling groups. This is most objectively disproved by the administration of sociometric tests, one at the beginning of the year, perhaps after two or three weeks of school, and another in the latter part of the school year. The sole prediction made (and with confidence) is that the grade line barriers will be crossed in many ways. Since the younger children of the primary groups will not likely be able to respond to the questions in written form, the tests will have to be given orally. If the services of a psychologist are available, this is within his province and, thus, this should be charged as his responsibility.

SUMMARY

No modern elementary school program can be managed well by the ill-prepared, unimaginative administrator. The dynamic instructional leader is an essential ingredient for successful implementation of new programs.

In the period of time immediately preceding the formal introduction of the ungraded school, the building principal must work intensively with his role; he must relate every teaching act, every aspect of curriculum, to the ungraded philosophy. It is also within his responsibility to properly orient non-instructional staff as well as children, particularly those initially affected. It is to his advantage to keep central administration informed of his activities and to solicit their assistance, as needed. All contingencies should be anticipated and planned for.

During the first official year of operation of the ungraded school, the building principal must be alert to all happenings. To accomplish this, he will be required to leave the sanctuary of his office, making frequent tours of all corners of his building, observing classrooms and corridors, teachers, parents, and pupils as they react to the new program. Interaction with staff should increase significantly. At the same time, the principal must accept the fact of increased teacher sensitivity. To a greater degree than ever, the principal should enact the role of the resource person, able and willing to give real assistance to the teacher.

Keeping a written record of experience in dealing with the various pieces of the new program, the principal will be in a better position to guide the evolving program, and to report to the other professionals in the district in the most enlightening terms.

The sociometric test for the interage class should help to dispel some of the unexpressed fears regarding that portion of the ungraded concept.

10

Some Summary Statements
... and a Look
Ahead

The ungraded elementary school is indeed the school of the immediate future for our nation. For some, it is the school of today. How remarkable it is that the fetters of the graded school, hammered out of Prussian logic so long ago, have constrained educational progress in our country for so long a time. Against the background of modern day progress, it is a classic example of a foolish anachronism.

Why hasn't public education made progress? One large piece of the blame may rest with our much-prized local control, which allows the farmer in the dell more authority in school matters, at times, than the individual who has devoted a lifetime to the profession. This, however, is a topic of considerable magnitude which cannot be given adequate treatment in a paragraph or two of this chapter.

The prevailing superficial impression among large segments of the uninitiated is that the ungraded school is a specific kind of "gimmick," one that can be imitated easily and precisely by following step one and two and three. It is hoped that this book has succeeded in emphasizing that the ungraded school is a modern philosophy, that one of the advantages of it being a philosophy is in the flexibility it permits for local adoption. Yet, as such, it cannot be an incidental program. Every school activity should feel the effects of the concept.

If the development of an ungraded program is to be undertaken by a school or school district, it should be recognized that the success of the endeavor will be determined largely by the extent and the quality of the preparatory activity. Further, it must be considered a team effort to which staff members on every level contribute. Throughout, the leadership ought to be bright and inspirational, and the leader must be tireless. To ignore the power of the community is unwise. Some lay involvement is necessary, particularly in the early stages, and a well-plotted program of selling might be designed a la Madison Avenue.

In-service training of teaching staff, well before the formal introduction of the ungraded program, will insure a base of understanding by the staff of the ideas inherent in the ungraded philosophy. The type and the extent of the training required will depend upon local needs, identified by a thorough period of self-investigation.

A program of supervision is necessary in order to properly service a program of instruction. The supervisor can be effective only if his background and administrative skill are commensurate to the task.

There are some tools of instruction available which make these distant goals somewhat easier to reach. Some of the programmed materials available show considerable promise. The buyer must be wary, of course, of the many high-cost, low-performance materials on the market which advertise glibly, using the recognized terminology, but which are otherwise poor imitations.

SOME FINAL RECOMMENDATIONS

These final recommendations pertain particularly to those schools on the verge of the new venture and already beyond the preliminaries. Some of the suggestions may be repetitious; however, the intent is to place these closer together and in a more orderly pattern.

The Gradual Approach

The majority of the districts which have put the ungraded plan into effect proceeded slowly in the development of their plan. In those instances where a school moved rapidly, there were expressions of some regret caused by public reaction. To avoid this, all efforts should be made gradually. The degree of success of the program will depend largely upon the acceptance by teaching staff and community. "Radical departure" or "upheaval" tends to threaten the security of these groups. The advocates of change for improvement must initially be content with the salesman's basic rule number one: Get that foot in the door!

Role of the Superintendent

The school superintendent, as the educational leader of a community, is essentially the key figure in bringing about educational change. He need not always be the initiator of a particular program, but his support is of paramount importance. Griffiths, describing his "systems theory of administrative change" notes:

> Many organizations bring in outsiders as administrators believing that change for the better will result. This apparently works in many cases. . . . All organizations exhibit some form of progressive segregation or hierarchial order. The order makes it possible for change to occur from the top down and practically impossible from the bottom up.[1]

---

[1] Daniel E. Griffiths, *The Job Performance of School Administrators: A Research Development Project,* New York: Teachers College, Columbia University, p. 41.

It is appropriate at this point to quote the experience of one elementary principal whose school, for some time, was alone in having an ungraded program:

> We were left to go it alone for almost ten years. A new superintendent came along and suggested that all participate . . . and they did.

Accepting Griffith's contention, supported by the principal's comment, it is recommended that the superintendent demonstrate his support and enthusiasm for the proposed program through the application of whatever reasonable measures are at his disposal and to the degree necessary to insure reasonable success. The recommendation is *not* that the superintendent exert pressure to initiate the program in all schools simultaneously, for this is contrary to the recommendation for gradual movement; simply, it is that he take an active interest in the project and demonstrate support for it.

Which Schools Participate?

In a district where there are several elementary schools, and where it is agreed that all will not participate simultaneously, the superintendent must decide how best to proceed. When the leadership for ungrading has come from a particular principal, the decision to allow that principal's school to move first is obvious enough.

School districts generally have found it most practical to begin the innovation in one school. The decisions to incorporate other schools would be based, in large part, one the experiences—the successes, the failures, the omissions, the overplays—of that pilot school. Moveover, unanticipated problems could be attacked and resolved with less complication when they are isolated in the one school.

After that year of trial, other schools would be invited to move into the formalized ungraded program. By constant referral to *formalized* program, I wish to acknowledge that all schools are on the road to complete adoption of the ungraded program, inasmuch as all schools, if there is a thread of unity in the district, must operate under the same philosophy. Central administration must take it plain enough that it tolerates degrees of difference between schools but that, ultimately, school *system* implies unity of goals, especially in the long range category, and educational progress in the same direction.

On this matter, the statesmanship of the chief school administrator is exercised. A snorting bull may intimidate the building underlings, but the unenthusiastic subordinates may do harm to a fine idea. To wait and hope for acceptance somehow, someday, is not enough; yet participation must be voluntary.

Action will stem from need and will be facilitated by sound information. Building principals and staff, if they are aware of the need to fully implement the philosophy of the district, will welcome opportunities to accomplish this to the furthest degree possible. With information provided them on the formal program, they will be able to determine their own readiness for the program. Thus, even while the plan is in operation in the pilot school that first year, the primary staff and the building principals of all the elementary schools of the district should receive a thorough orientation. This would take place during the early part of the school year, perhaps in November, and might include some visitation to the pilot school. It must be noted again that the ungraded school as such, is not dramatically visible. The reason for the visit would be to point this out to the visitors, to help underline the fact that it is only another logical step in the direction of the district goals.

Following the orientation, and the limited visitation, the staff members of the other schools, together with their building principals, would carry on full discussions of the plan. Finally, they would render their decisions on the matter of participation through the building principal. Where there is less than eager acceptance, the policy should discourage participation.

Which Labels to Remove?

It is usual for districts to begin their formal ungrading program by eliminating the designation of grades 1 through 3. This procedure enables a program of grouping which produces a reasonable degree of refinement in pupil placement. Classes are ordinarily referred to as Mrs. Blank's primary class, Miss Clark's primary class, etc. On occasion there may be reason to indicate that a class is composed of first year primary students, or second year primary students, or that the class is interage, composed of first and second year primary students, or second and third year primary students. In most cases, however, it is sufficient to identify a class by the teacher.

Depending upon experience, a decision would have to be made regarding the incorporation of grade 4 into the ungraded unit in the following year. Referring to the experience of many of the pioneer districts, we can note that many were content for many years simply to have an ungraded primary. With time, the trend is to ungrade all of the elementary grades and, in some instances, the secondary school. This must be a local decision based upon local conditions. It appears indecisive and uncourageous to have both graded and ungraded units within a school after a school has had a number of years to decide that they have or have not succeeded in their mission. If grade designations are barriers at one level, they are barriers at other levels. While I have preached a degree of caution and gradualism (for which I have been criticised by some), I believe that long periods of inaction are unjustifiable.

A Question of Time

The building principal cannot escape the question: Which children will be served best by giving them an additional year in school or, as they say in Athens, Georgia, given "an extended opportunity?" These youngsters given the additional year must never be conceded as retentions. Children are not left back. They are not repeating what they failed to learn. Instead, they had been allowed to move at the pace that fits them best, according to their style and manner of learning. They had been spared the frustrations and humiliations of daily hour-by-hour failure. The decision to "permit" the slower pace, to develop their programs according to their abilities, was an enlightened concession to reality, was in the best interests of the children involved, therefore justifiable and good. The results of this policy are better-than-otherwise students, academically, and probably socially and psychologically.

When the decision is rendered to give a child an additional year that child should understand the concept of continuous progress. More flexible than their parents, less concerned with the symbols of status, they are likely to accept the explanation and the decision. Their degree of acceptance will, of course, influence their parents.

Is it ever proper to penalize a child for learning at a rapid pace by depriving him of a year of schooling? I must contend that it is a rather strange reward. Yet we are often faced with this problem. The decision to cut off a year of time is most frequently accepted with ease and pleasure. That, in itself, is no reason for the decision.

In logic, the better alternative, if it exists, is to provide the proper kind of program without having to cut off a year of instruction. Instead of a shorter time of instruction for some, perhaps a better goal is a longer program. However, this ought not to be interpreted as "a lot more of the same." High Schools are now, in some instances, featuring advanced placement classes as a means of coping with the problem of the unchallenged. This is the better direction.

A Summation of Recommendations

After the decision to begin a formal ungraded program, the

initiating district must face a sequence of questions related to their decision. In this chapter and throughout the book, recommendations have dealt with many of these questions. The following are some of the more obvious guidelines:

1. In adopting an ungraded school, the changes that are required or found desirable should be made gradually and cautiously.

2. The district superintendent (or chief school administrator), as the most important agent for change, should demonstrate full support and enthusiasm for the program.

3. One school only should be designated as the pilot school for the first year of operation.

4. Participation of other schools, in following years, should be voluntary; decisions on this should be rendered through the building principal.

5. In the first year, the first three grades should be replaced.

6. During the second year, a determination should be made, as a result of study, as to whether or not additional grades should undergo the ungrading process.

7. The new policy on retention and acceleration would be made known to all concerned, particularly those characteristics which distinguish it from the "left back" and "skipped" aspects of the old policy.

8. The elementary reading consultant, or other such specialist, should work with the kindergarten teachers during the last several weeks of school in order to standardize pupil evaluation, particularly as related to pupil placement for the new school year.

9. Readiness tests are recommended for administration to first year of primary students within five weeks of the first day of school; other primary students would be tested with other standardized tests. The informal reading inventory is an excellent determiner of real reading level.

10. Each class should have social and academic leaders; problem children should be equally distributed; no isolates should be kept in a class if different placement can resolve the matter; reading groups should be limited to three, these being contiguous.

11. Teachers of the lower levels should have the smaller class sizes.

12. During the first year of operation, meetings between the primary teachers and building administration should be held with relative frequency.

13. A meeting of primary teachers, building administration, school psychologist, and reading consultant should be held at the end of the first five week period for the purpose of refining grouping. Necessary changes would be made. Throughout the year, thereafter, changes would be made as necessary, although there is no reason to anticipate large numbers of these changes.

14. A full program of orientation should be provided for: the elementary principals, the primary teachers, and the parents whose children would participate in the program. Special provisions should be made for the new primary staff (those coming in without the benefit of full orientation).

15. A program of familiarization should be provided for those staff members who are not directly involved in the beginning years.

16. The reporting system should be modified to include formal parent-teacher conferences and anecdotal reporting.

A LOOK AHEAD

Taking A Chance On Change

One thing certain about change is that it entails risk. While we can anticipate improved achievement for pupils, lessening of tensions for children and staff . . . and all of the other benefits which the experiences of others have proved possible, we also realize the immense effort required.

It is easier not to initiate change. The innovator is, often enough, held suspect by too many adults who should know better. Bit of a pest, he is, and he will pay a price.

The mature, serious, informed, and conscientious educator has little choice. He has a low tolerance for the obvious deficiencies of the educational instruments that he is forced to use . . . temporarily. Problems beware!

Officials of the school or school district that becomes ungraded frequently feel that they must evaluate and prove the value of the new plan. There are instruments that measure some of the educational products, but there are many aspects that are seldom measured adequately: attitudes, morale, community understanding. Much measuring must be subjective. This is no terrible flaw which ought to promote guilt feelings. It has seldom been proposed that the graded structure be scientifically scrutinized and justified.

The effectiveness of the ungraded plan depends upon people. This plan, for that matter, any instrument of education is of little consequence by itself. It is the human personality that possesses the magic ingredients which have the power to transform an idea and a hope into a creative, functioning force. The injection of enthusiasm, the application of human ingenuity can very well determine and insure the success of an enterprise; conversely, the withholding of support, the human rejection of the most elaborately conceived and cleverly designed implement must destroy its potential.

We cannot deny that the ungraded plan is subject to the profound influence of the individuals who would relate to it. Those individuals most directly involved bear the greatest burden in the determination of its success. They, in turn, require the cooperation of all of those individuals less directly involved.

Change demands effort. It may cause some anxiety that must

come of probing the unknown or unfamiliar. Justifiable and desirable change, however, is essential to any profession that expects to keep pace with a rapidly-progressing society. Education has no choice, which means the educator has no choice, no alternative, when society thrusts him into a leadership role. After a long period of second class citizenship, the spotlight shines brightly upon the educator. Will he behave like a second class citizen, settle upon his 3 R's comfortably? I think not.

SOME PREDICTIONS

The elementary school of the future, and not the far-away future, is going to be ungraded. Teachers will seek to develop programs for each of their pupils. Perhaps better than the term ungraded we can refer to such schools as *pupil-programmed.*

Textbook publishers and all of those commercial organizations which supply the schools with the varied instructional materials are bound to perceive the irreversible trend and they will begin to develop their materials accordingly. It was true in the past that the textbook publishers helped to bind education tightly to the grade structure. By accommodating the pupil-programmed school, they will sever the rusted Prussian-style shackles.

The instructor who is only a step or two ahead of his pupils, whose plan of instruction seldom goes beyond telling his pupils the "right" information, is now fading from the scene . . . because he doesn't belong. Throughout this book it has been pointed out that the teacher must expend large quantities of additional time and effort to effect those changes which can be so promising. It can be done. Incidentally, this social situation is not without a touch of humor. While electricians and production workers and industry in general move in the direction of "teacher's hours", the teacher's work week increases . . . the result of professional-quality instruction.

What will be the teacher's reward for all of this? Salaries must be increased dramatically, and not only in the gold coast sections of the country. The purse-string holders have a fight on their hands if they intend to evade their responsibilities in this matter. Witness the footholds of the teacher unions, the surge of militancy in the heretofore slow-moving, overcautious professional organizations.

But what does this have to do with the ungrading of schools? Re-phrased, the question becomes: Is there a relationship between the quality of a school program and the salaries paid the teachers who are expected to help develop and to implement the program? The answer: The effective ungraded school calls for a quality of staff that would not be attracted to unattractive salaries.

As schools increase the quality of their performance, the overwhelming influence of the taxpayer will lessen. For every irate table-thumper there will be a dozen supporters to intercede in behalf of the schools. Additionally, competent educators are apt to demonstrate the courage to resist the noisier layman.

There is a dark spot in this brightly optimistic outlook. The much-cherished system of local control, extolled as a feature of our democracy, does, in fact, promote waste through unnecessary duplication and through lack of standardization. Also, there is something disquietingly foolish in the fact that adjoining communities may have systems of education starkly contrasting.

All things considered, at every level of our democracy education is being recognized as a cornerstone for the building of a better society. And the grip of gradedness has been broken.

Appendix A

THE QUESTIONNAIRE AND A SUMMARY OF RESPONSES

Prior to initiating the ungraded school in Central School District No. 4, the author developed a questionnaire which he submitted to the forty-four "pioneer" school districts identified in Goodlad and Anderson's, THE NONGRADED ELEMENTARY SCHOOL published by Harcourt, Brace & Company. Thirty-six of those districts responded. Following are summations of those responses, including comments. Items thoroughly covered elsewhere in the text are omitted here.

ITEMS CONCERNED WITH IMPLEMENTATION
OF THE PLAN

Which procedures were used to orient the teaching staff that were to be involved in the implementation plan?

( ) A written guide   ( ) Staff meetings

( ) Bulletins   ( ) Other . . . If other, please
                                       explain.

All responses to the above question indicated the use of staff meetings for purposes of orientation. In seven instances, staff meetings were used exclusively; in nine of the responding districts, more than two procedures were used.

Several methods of orientation were described under "Other." These included: (1) meetings with the County Council (Tampa, Fla.); (2) workshops in a pilot school (Vestal, N.Y.); (3) bringing in consultants (Douglas, Ga.); (4) visits to other ungraded schools (Grosse Point Woods, Mich., Waukeegan, Ill., Moline, Ill.); (5) joint committees with parents (Cabool, Mo.).

Major implication: Face-to-face meetings were considered essential for developing staff orientation. Various other procedures were used, but were used, generally, to add to the effectiveness of the staff meeting.

Was a written guide developed to describe the program? If so, who devised it?

( ) Yes The author(s): ( ) Central Administration
( ) No   ( ) Building principal(s)
                              ( ) Combined effort of_____
                              ( ) Other—please specify_____

Of the twenty-three communities that developed a guide, the largest number, fourteen, were devised through the joint efforts of building administration and faculty. In only one stated instance were parents included in the development of the instrument. In five communities, committees of teachers were given full credit for the guide, while in four districts the members of central administration were identified as the sole authors.

Major finding: The surveyed districts generally favored the development of a guide and by their comments indicated that this was best accomplished through the team efforts of building administration and teaching staff.

What was the make-up of the meetings held in planning for the new program?
( ) Teachers directly involved and the building principal
( ) All the teachers of the building and the building principal
( ) Other . . . please describe:_____
How frequently were these meetings held preceding the formal initiation of the program?

In about half of the responding communities, the staff meetings were composed solely of the teachers directly involved and the building principal. In four instances, the meetings were held with the primary teachers, building principal, and one other individual or group, as follows: (1) an intermediate staff representative, (2) primary supervisors, (3) fourth grade teachers, and (4) an occasional visit by the district superintendent.

Ten communities noted a variety of combinations. Most frequent was the notation that the meetings at first included only the teachers directly involved and that, as time went on, full staff was included in the planning. In some cases the meetings included parents, consultants, and psychologists. When several schools were involved in the transition there were some system-wide meetings.

Major findings: The meetings concerned with the specific development of the ungraded plan began, in most cases, with a nucleus of those individuals who were directly involved. As the study progressed and the plan evolved, others were brought into the planning group, either as participants or observers.

Regarding the matter of frequency of meetings, it was found that most districts, once having committed themselves, chose to meet formally once a week. Total number of meetings ranged from one (this district soon discontinued the plan) to thirty-six. In nearly all of the communities, the meetings were held within that year preceding formal adoption of the ungraded plan.

What procedures were used to orient new staff to the philosophy and
application of the ungraded plan? Check all applicable statements.
( ) Written guide given for   ( ) Assignment of "buddy" teach-
    study   er
( ) Special conferences for new   ( ) Other . . . please describe
    staff

All but three of the responding communities provided for formal orientation conferences for new staff members. Another frequently used device was the written guide. About 70% used the
technique of the assignment of a "buddy" teacher. Most communities used one or more procedures in addition to formal
conferences.

Included among "other" were: (1) continuing assistance of
building principal, (2) meetings with helping teachers, (3) continuous assistance of consultants, (4) pre-school orientation,
(5) workshops, and (6) pre-employment visitation within the system.

Major implications: (1) The majority of districts used more
than one procedure for orienting new staff, nearly all of which
included formal conferences, and (2) there was considerable
dependence on written materials in communicating procedures
to new teachers.

Since the implementation of the plan, has your experience revealed
that certain phases of pre-planning were most effective, while others
could have been improved?

Most effective_____
Might have been improved_____
Comments: _____

Following are representative comments describing the most
effective procedures:

1. We encouraged maximum teacher participation.
2. We included key PTA parents in our initial planning.
3. Our regularly-held conferences were most effective.
4. We developed and interpreted to staff and parents a common philosophy.
5. Most important were the planning sessions with the primary teachers.
6. There is no one best procedure.
7. Our determination to proceed slowly was our best idea.
8. Our success has been due to fluid communication.
9. The teacher-principal involvement was of the greatest importance.
10. Our grouping to maintain continuous progress was the most effective procedure.
11. Most helpful were our parent meetings with teachers, as were the parent-principal meetings.
12. We believe that our small staff group meetings were the most helpful.
13. Our consideration of time-staff was not rushed headlong into this.

Significantly, nearly all of the comments relative to "might have been improved" touched upon the tender matter of community relations. These were reported in the chapter on community relations. In general, districts felt they could have or should have better prepared the community.

Outside of public-relations, these comments were made:

1. We might have explained the plan city-wide and then called for volunteers to work with it. A volunteer will always do better than a teacher who feels the plan was imposed on her.
2. We could have improved our grading and our reporting of pupil progress.
3. We didn't have a specially designated person to work with teachers during the year. We have now found this to be essential.

ITEM ON COMPETITION

The ungraded plan has served to:

( ) eliminate competition   ( ) reduce competition to a large
( ) reduce competition to   extent
    some extent   ( ) has not affected to competitive
Comments: aspects of school life

___

There were twenty-eight responses to this item, ten of which indicated that the ungraded plan did not affect the competitive aspects of school life. Two communities stated that competition was eliminated. One of these qualified the statement by noting that "unfair" competition had been eliminated. Ten other responses selected the choice "reduced competition to a large extent"; six selected the choice, "to some extent."

Following are representative comments:

1. It has reduced *frustration*.
2. Competition among equals or individually is not undesirable.
3. We have tried to eliminate competition but it is inevitable.
4. We have eliminated *failure*, but not competition.
5. It has changed the focus of competition to put it in better perspective.
6. The school has a large number of professional parents of high socio-economic levels and who are highly ambitious for their children.
7. Children are still competing but much more realistically. More of them feel they have a chance now.
8. There is a chance for leadership now. . .there's wholesome competition.

ITEMS ON REPORTING AND RECORD KEEPING

Has the use of the ungraded plan necessitated the revision of your system of reporting to parents?

( ) Yes   If a change was required, what particular aspect of the
( ) No   reporting system needed revision?

_____

What written records needed major revision as a result of operating the
ungraded plan? Please identify:

_____
=======================================

Of the thirty-one replies to these items, only four communities
marked "no" to the question pertaining to the need for revision
of the reporting system. Thirteen respondents indicated the need
for the inclusion of parent conferences as part of their reporting
system. The comments of explanation underlined the importance
of this reporting device in developing parental understanding of
the new program. Following are representative comments:

1. We introduced the designation of reading and arithmetic
   achievement levels, as well as parent conferences.
2. Report cards are given to parents at individual conferences.
3. We have many more group and individual conferences
   to explain our program as it applies to individual children.
   We have developed a card of some detail to supplement
   conferences.
4. The traditional report card has been changed to letters
   (essay reporting), notes, and parent-teacher conferences.
5. We began using narrative reporting. . .supplemented by
   conferences.
6. There is much more reliance on parent-teacher conferences
   and group meetings with parents.
7. We eliminated the damnable report cards and went to the
   conference method.
8. Bulletin and conference reporting had been added to regular card reporting to insure that parents understood the
   child's progress level and rate of progress.
9. Evaluation is done in reference to potential rather than by
   age-grade standards.

10. There has been a change in the philosophy of reporting progress as well as changes in the card itself.

Eight of the responding communities felt no need to revise anything other than the report card. Fourteen communities had need to revise the cumulative records of the individual pupil; many of those noted that the change necessary was slight.

ITEMS ON RETENTION AND ACCELERATION

What is the experience of your system regarding the retention of a child in the primary section for an additional year? Give numbers, if available, or a statement of description.

A number of respondents took the opportunity to note displeasure with the term "retention." Some terms preferred were: "an extended year. . .an opportunity," . . ."retardation without repeating." Another comment: "Some children require an extra year, but this is hardly retention."

Following are some of the comments made in response to the question:

1. Very few are retained. Some immature pupils made surprising gains as they matured. . .who would otherwise have been retained.
2. Only a few children get an extended year.
3. There are fewer "retentions" than under graded system. Most seem to catch up.
4. Roughly 10% now spend an extra year. This is fewer than before.
5. This has gone down to about 2%.
6. We do this at the end of the sixth year, with parent approval. In our first year all parents turned us down.
7. The number of retentions has been cut in half.

Since the ungraded plan was initiated, have any children been "accelerated" (kept in the ungraded section less than the average period of time)?

There are differences of opinion on whether "acceleration" is desirable. Marshall C. Jameson, principal of an ungraded school at Grosse Pointe Woods, Michigan, at the time of the survey depicts the process as "cheating a child out of a year of elementary school." In another district, an official bemoaned the fact that there weren't as many accelerations as there might if class sizes were smaller.

Following are some representative comments:

1. We accelerated very few, mostly girls.
2. We have tried some accelerations. There would be more with classes of 25 or less.
3. Only a very small number are accelerated.
4. We did some, but we changed. Why cheat a child?
5. There are no accelerations in our system.
6. Many have gone through our primary program in 2½ years.

Appendix B

A SAMPLE LETTER SENT TO PARENTS AFTER ROOM
ASSIGNMENTS WERE MADE FOR THE FIRST YEAR OF
THE FORMALLY UNGRADED PROGRAM

Parkway School
June 30

Dear Parents:

In anticipation of your questions, I wish to make comment on room assignments for the coming year. For some, there may be concern with that facet of our ungraded program which promotes some interage classes. Also, teachers who were identified formerly with a particular grade may now be assigned to different age groups.

It is important that you appreciate certain facts about our program. I list these for your understanding:

The program about to go into operation has been studied intensively during the past two years. It is a natural outgrowth of our district's present programs and is intended to benefit the children. Dozens of communities throughout the United States have had many years of successful experience with the ungraded plan. All have claimed important educational gains for the children involved.

The success of *any* program hinges almost entirely upon the quality of the staff involved. I claim, without reservation, that the Parkway staff are highly competent and that their skills will insure the successful incorporation of the ungraded plan.

The possible advantages and disadvantages of our new program have been seriously weighed. Only after the most comprehensive reporting of facts was the approval given to proceed. This approval was given after presentation to faculty, to school administration, to central administration, and finally to the board of education.

Already we have reaped certain definite advantages:

1. Class size has been controlled.
2. Imminent retentions have been avoided.
3. Grouping for greater instructional efficiency has been achieved.

We must have your support and confidence if we are going to succeed in our determination to offer your children the best kind of educational program. Bear in mind the quality of staff is, by far, the most important factor in any kind of program and that our intent is to constantly evaluate and improve our educational practices.

But—your confidence and support is of considerable value to us.

Sincerely,

Frank R. Dufay
Principal, Parkway School

Appendix C

THE FORM LETTER SENT TO PARENTS TO ADVISE THEM OF CHANGE IN CLASS ASSIGNMENT IN EARLY PART OF SCHOOL YEAR

Dear Parents:

Your child, ..., is being transferred from Room No. .... to Room No. ...., ...'s class, effective ....

If you will read the explanation following, we believe you will understand and appreciate the necessity for the move.

All classes in Parkway School have been put together on the basis of a very definite grouping plan. The purpose of the grouping plan is to provide the classroom teacher with the best possible teaching situation and, for the children, the best possible learning situation.

Our plan insures that each class has pupil leadership, that problems of any kind are equitably distributed, and that there is a maximum reading range of three levels of achievement. At the beginning of each year we double-check our grouping to insure that proper pupil placement has been achieved. When we discover a need to change pupil placement, despite some minor inconveniences involved, we make the changes. The sole purpose of these changes is to provide the pupil with the best possible learning situation. We have done this each year and we have found this to be of important benefit. Our intention is to avoid the hardships imposed on pupil and teacher when a pupil is not properly placed.

I suggest that you take the time, some two weeks or so after the change has been effected, to meet with your child's teacher in order to exchange information on his progress. Your cooperation will make the transition smooth and pleasant.

Please feel free to call my office if you wish additional information.

Sincerely,

Frank R. Dufay, Principal

Appendix D

(Distributed to staff in the early part of the first year of the ungraded program.)

To: Faculty
From: Principal
Re: Standardization references to the ungraded program

In dealing with our Greater Cleveland math, we appreciate the need for standardizing our math language. The same holds true in medicine, law, as in other professions and trades.

Regarding our ungraded program, let us consider these acceptable terms:

We have placed our grades (1, 2, 3) with an *ungraded primary unit*. There are sixteen *primary classes*. The children in the primary unit, in any of the primary classes, are not first graders, second graders, or third graders, but are *primary pupils* in the primary unit. In certain situations, when there is reason and need for identification, pupils may be termed *first year pupils, second year pupils, third year pupils* and, in some instances, *fourth year pupils*. All primary teachers are *primary teachers*. When necessary they may be identified as *teachers of first year students, teachers of second year students, teachers of third year students, teachers of first and second year students, teachers of second and third year students.*

Levels are used only in reference to academic achievement. A primary pupil may be at one level in arithmetic, another in reading. We use levels in grouping children but these are not valid in identification of any particular class. There is no second level class or teacher or pupil.

Please,

Let us spend the necessary effort in using the proper terminology. We do have the program. It is a sound one. There is good reason for it. Let us do a fine job in all respects.

Frank R. Dufay, Principal

Appendix E

Questionnaire For Parents of Maple Park School, Edmonds, Wash.

QUESTIONNAIRE ON UNGRADED PRIMARY

Questions may be answered by a simple yes or no and in some cases by a check mark. Space has been left between each question to allow for comments in case you feel you need to qualify your answer. Any general comments you wish to make, not related to a question asked, can be made on the reverse side.

1. Do you feel you have a good understanding of how your child will progress through the Primary School.

   Yes 162   No 45   No response 6

2. Do you feel that the school placed your child in the proper level?

   Yes 201   No 8   No response 22

   If your answer is No: Too high   Too low

3. Do you feel that your child has progressed, so far satisfactorily?

   Yes 190   No 23   No response 11

4. Do you feel that your child would have made more progress had he remained in a graded system?

   Yes 20   No 158   No response 35

5. Do you feel it is a problem to your child in shifting from teacher to teacher?

   Yes   70   No   123   No response   24

6. Do you feel that there should be a clearer indication of the level the child is working in?

   Yes   111   No   96   No response _____

7. Do you feel that your child is getting more individual attention?

   Yes   146   No   42   No response   34

8. Do you feel that the explanation of the program at the meetings held last fall was adequate?

   Yes   137   No   29   No response   56

9. Have you noticed a change in your child's attitude towards school since the change in the program?

   Yes   107   No   29   No response   16

   If your answer is yes, check one: Improved   79   Poorer   23

10. If your child left Maple Park do you feel it would be a problem entering him in another school?

    Yes   56   No   135   No response   26

11. If you were given another opportunity to vote on the Primary School would you vote?

    Yes   167   No   28   No response   26

    If this is a change from your previous vote, please explain.

Index